BARTH, ISRAEL, AND JESUS

Very little has been written on Barth's doctrine of Israel in the later volumes of the Church Dogmatics; *and Barth's view of the state of Israel is one that will prove as timely – and controversial – as it did in Barth's own day. Professor Lindsay's prose is clear and literate, always welcome in this field. Volume 4 of the* Church Dogmatics *is the major re-statement of Christology in our era, and the place Jews and the people of Israel have in those volumes should be of interest to all Barth scholars and theologians who work in Christology.*

Professor Kate Sonderegger, Virginia Theological Seminary, USA

Following his earlier analysis of Barth's theological critique of Nazi antisemitism in 'Covenanted Solidarity', Mark Lindsay turns to examine the significance of the holocaust for Barth's post-war theology of Israel, particularly in the doctrine of reconciliation. Lucidly written, with scrupulous attention to the scope and the details of the texts, this is Barth scholarship of a high order, and will also be read with profit by all concerned for the relations of Christians and Jews.

Professor John Webster, King's College, Aberdeen

It is splendid to welcome Mark Lindsay's latest book. With his rigorous attention to the diverse contexts of Barth's long theological journey, Lindsay persuasively argues that the Shoah *and the establishment of the modern state of Israel are proper subjects of theology and shows how they entered into and gave form to Barth's late work. Highly relevant and helpful for current reflection on Jewish–Christian relations and providing a refreshing perspective on Karl Barth's contextuality makes this one of the best studies on Barth today.*

Martin Rumscheidt, Atlantic School of Theology, Nova Scotia, Canada

The attitude of Karl Barth to Israel and the Jews has long been the subject of heated controversy amongst historians and theologians. The question that has so far predominated in the debate has been Barth's attitude, both theologically and practically, towards the Jews during the period of the Third Reich and the Holocaust itself. How, if at all, did Barth's attitudes change in the post-war years? Did Barth's own theologising in the aftermath of the Holocaust take that horrendous event into account in his later writings on Israel and the Jews? Mark Lindsay explores such questions through a deep consideration of volume four of Barth's *Church Dogmatics*, the 'Doctrine of Reconciliation'.

Barth Studies

Series Editors

John Webster, Professor of Theology, University of Aberdeen, UK
George Hunsinger, Director of the Center for Barth Studies,
Princeton University, USA
Hans-Anton Drewes, Director of the Karl Barth Archive, Basel, Switzerland

The work of Barth is central to the history of modern western theology and remains a major voice in contemporary constructive theology. His writings have been the subject of intensive scrutiny and re-evaluation over the past two decades, notably on the part of English-language Barth scholars who have often been at the forefront of fresh interpretation and creative appropriation of his theology. Study of Barth, both by graduate students and by established scholars, is a significant enterprise; literature on him and conferences devoted to his work abound; the Karl Barth Archive in Switzerland and the Center for Barth Studies at Princeton give institutional profile to these interests. Barth's work is also considered by many to be a significant resource for the intellectual life of the churches.

Drawing from the wide pool of Barth scholarship, and including translations of Barth's works, this series aims to function as a means by which writing on Barth, of the highest scholarly calibre, can find publication. The series builds upon and furthers the interest in Barth's work in the theological academy and the church.

Barth, Israel, and Jesus

Karl Barth's Theology of Israel

MARK R. LINDSAY
*University of Melbourne, Australia
and University of St Andrews, UK*

ASHGATE

Published by
Ashgate Publishing Limited
Gower House
Croft Road
Aldershot
Hampshire GU11 3HR
England

Ashgate Publishing Company
Suite 420
101 Cherry Street
Burlington, VT 05401-4405
USA

Ashgate website: http://www.ashgate.com

British Library Cataloguing in Publication Data
Lindsay, Mark R., 1971–
  Barth, Israel, and Jesus : Karl Barth's theology of Israel. – (Barth studies)
  1. Barth, Karl, 1886–1968 2. Israel (Christian theology) 3. Christianity and other religions – Judaism – 1945–
  I. Title
  231.7'6'092

Library of Congress Cataloging-in-Publication Data
Lindsay, Mark R., 1971–
  Barth, Israel, and Jesus : Karl Barth's theology of Israel / Mark R Lindsay.
      p. cm.—(Barth studies) Includes bibliographical references and index.
  1. Barth, Karl, 1886–1968. 2. Christianity and other religions—Judaism—1945–
  3. Judaism—Relations—Christianity—1945– 4. Barth, Karl, 1886–1968. Lehre von der Versvhnung. 5. Reconciliation—Religious aspects—Christianity. 6. Holocaust (Christian theology) 7. Israel—History—Religious aspects—Christianity. I. Title.

  BX4827.B3L56 2007
  261.2'6092—dc22

                                                                      2006018458

ISBN 978-0-7546-5087-4

Printed and bound in Great Britain by MPG Books Ltd, Bodmin, Cornwall.

'Your name will be Israel, because you have struggled
with God and with men and have overcome.'

—Gen 32:28

Contents

Preface

As is the lot of many younger scholars, the joy of seeing my doctoral dissertation published in late 2001 was tempered by the realization that I had completed merely the first instalment of what, if the job was to be done properly, could only be at least a two-part study. Now with the second part completed, I find myself part of what can only be described as something of a renaissance in Barth scholarship. The recently-established Online Bibliography of Karl Barth—a joint venture between the Center for Barth Studies at Princeton and the Theological University of Kampen in the Netherlands—is ample evidence of this renaissance, with new and exciting contributions being made in recent years from every part of the world. Similarly, in 2006 Princeton Theological Seminary and the Karl Barth Society of North America hosted the inaugural 'Annual Karl Barth Conference'. Everywhere, it seems, Barth scholarship (and appreciation) is on the increase. The small addition of this book will serve, I trust, a double purpose. As well as hopefully adding something of value to the existing scholarly literature on Barth's enduring theological legacy, it is my hope that through this book I will also be able to make a contribution—or better, show that Barth himself has already made a contribution—to the cause of Jewish–Christian dialogue.

Since 9/11, a great deal of theological effort has rightly gone into the delicate work of Christian–Muslim reconciliation. While undoubtedly a long-overdue and vitally necessary task, it remains my belief that the history of Jewish–Christian relations is in even more need of deep repair, largely because it has been a longer and (as we may tend to forget in light of recent experience) a far bloodier engagement. The anxiety that greeted the death of Pope John Paul II and the subsequent election of Benedict XVI, amongst those who have worked for so long toward better understanding between Christians and Jews, illustrated how fragile the relations still are. There are hopeful signs that Benedict's pontificate will not alter substantially the tremendous gains made under John Paul II. Nonetheless, progress in Jewish–Christian relations can never be taken for granted, and much work still needs to be done.

The role of Karl Barth—by general consensus the greatest Protestant theologian since Luther—in assisting or, in the view of his critics hindering, the reconciliation between Jews and Christians remains a contested subject. Given on the one hand the importance of seeking peace between these two faith traditions that between them account for some 2.5 billion people, and on the other hand Barth's stature within the theological world, it is vital that these two criteria of modern theology (I would argue that Barth's stature accords him status as a theological criterion) be brought into conversation. That is what this book aims to do, as a service both to interfaith dialogue and to Barth scholarship.

*

There are, as usual, many people to thank, without whose assistance this project would never have been finished. Sarah Lloyd at Ashgate has been invaluable from the start, with her encouragement, always timely advice, and wholehearted support of the book's validity. I can only offer humble apologies to her (and all the editorial team) that, in spite of my sincerest intentions, I found myself watching helplessly as deadlines came and went!

Martin Rumscheidt, albeit from the other side of the world, has been of greater encouragement to me than I can say. Ever since reading his analysis of the Barth-Harnack correspondence I have looked up to him as a scholar of the highest integrity and insight. I can think, therefore, of no greater compliment than to be called by him 'a fellow Barth scholar', and no one from whom such a compliment would mean more. I sincerely hope that this book does justice to his faith in me.

Paul Molnar, whose editorial advice was crucial to the completion of my first book, has continued to be a source of gracious and warm-hearted encouragement. I thank him most sincerely.

Ed Kessler, Lucia Faltin, Gwyneth Bodger, Melanie Wright—indeed all the staff, as well as my students, at the Centre for the Study of Jewish–Christian Relations in Cambridge; I am deeply grateful for the opportunity of spending four months with them in mid-2005 as the Sternberg Visiting Fellow in Interfaith Relations. Not only was it a wonderfully stimulating and enjoyable sabbatical, it also provided me with the time and space I needed to complete the research for this book. It would be remiss at this point to not also mention the many friends among the staff and students at Wesley House in Cambridge that I and my family made during our four months there: Fran, George and Adam Bailey, David and Ros Hollingsworth, Steven Plant, and Grant and Marie White, to name but a few. In particular, I must sincerely thank Sir Sigmund Sternberg, from whose generous benefaction my Cambridge fellowship was made possible.

While in the UK, I was privileged to accept invitations to speak on Barth and Bonhoeffer to seminar groups in the Divinity Schools of the Universities of Edinburgh and St Andrews. These presentations, and the questions raised by the students in response, were immensely helpful to me in tightening some of the key arguments I propose here. To Mario Aguilar (St Andrews), and David Fergusson, John McDowell and Jolyon Mitchell (Edinburgh), I am sincerely grateful.

Others who deserve heartfelt thanks for their advice and encouragement were mentioned in the preface to *Covenanted Solidarity*, but having continued to provide generous support need also to be mentioned here: especially, John Tonkin and John Conway. Were it not for them, neither this book nor its predecessor would ever have been written.

I wish also to record my gratitude to the Faculty at Whitley College, at the University of Melbourne, who have been wholeheartedly supportive of my research. Also, to my colleagues-in-ministry, and the congregation as a whole, at Essendon Baptist Church, among whom I am privileged to serve as a pastor.

My family, as always, has been wonderful. My wife Sonia, and my two boys Jack and Tom, have never failed to love and support me in my work, and have accepted with astonishing grace the insecurity with which the lives of young academics are all-too-often (and all-too-ruthlessly) burdened. Moreover, the pride with which my six-year-old son introduced me to his classmates as 'an author', and the entirely unwarranted awe with which they in turn received that news, was deeply humbling.

It is, then, perhaps superfluous—if never undeserved—to say that I owe to my family more than can be repaid.

Similarly, my in-laws, Philip and Suzy Thomas, have been a source of tremendous support and encouragement, notwithstanding the toll that my work has taken on their eldest daughter and grandsons.

To my uncle, Noel Vose, I am grateful. It is he who first instilled in me a love of theology, and more importantly taught me the necessity of using the theological task in the service of the Church.

Lastly, there were two of my family who I unconscionably overlooked in my first book, but whose encouragement, love and unfailing belief in me have been three immeasurably valuable constants throughout my life. And so, it is by way of loving but imperfect gratitude that I dedicate this book to my parents, Ian and Dawn.

Mark R. Lindsay, Melbourne

Acknowledgments

The author gratefully acknowledges receipt of permission to cite from the following:

Karl Barth, *Church Dogmatics*, eds G.W. Bromiley & T.F. Torrance, vols. III/3, IV/1, IV/2, IV/3.1, IV/3.2. Edinburgh: T & T Clark, 1936-1969.

Reprinted with kind permission of Continuum International Publishing Group. All rights reserved.

Letter, C. von Kirschbaum to Paul Vogt, 12 November 1938; 'Einladung', December 1938; Letter, C. von Kirschbaum to Paul Vogt, 27 January 1939; Letter, C. von Kirschbaum to Pfr. Rhenus Gelpke, 7 June 1939; Letter, K. Barth to E. Nobs, 25 June 1944; Letter, K. Barth *et al* to the Swiss Federal Council, 4 July 1944. All from the Karl Barth-Archiv, Basel.

Reprinted by permission from the Karl Barth-*Stiftung* (Basel, Switzerland). All rights reserved.

The author also acknowledges with grateful thanks receipt of the following, without which the writing of the book would have been made far more difficult:

Sternberg Visiting Fellowship in Interfaith Relations, Centre for the Study of Jewish–Christian Relations, Wesley House, Cambridge.

List of Abbreviations

CD   Karl Barth, *Church Dogmatics*, 4 vols, 13 parts, ed. and trans. G.W. Bromiley & T.F. Torrance, (Edinburgh: T & T Clark, 1936–1969).

GD   Karl Barth, *The Göttingen Dogmatics: Instruction in the Christian Religion*, vol.1, trans. G.W. Bromiley, ed. H. Reiffen, (Grand Rapids: Eerdmans, 1991).

GS   Dietrich Bonhoeffer, *Gesammelte Schriften*, 6 vols, ed. E. Bethge, (Munich: Christian Kaiser Verlag, 1954–78).

IJST   *International Journal of Systematic Theology.*

LPP   Dietrich Bonhoeffer, *Letters and Papers from Prison*, ed. E. Bethge, (London: SCM Press, 1971).

Rom I   Karl Barth, *Der Römerbrief*, erste Fassung, (G.A. Bäschlin, 1919; repr. Zürich: TVZ, 1985).

Rom II   Karl Barth, *Der Römerbreif*, zweite Fassung, (Munich: Christian Kaiser Verlag, 1922); ET The Epistle to the Romans, trans. E.C. Hoskyns, (London: Oxford University Press, 1933).

SJT   *Scottish Journal of Theology.*

WGWM   Karl Barth, *The Word of God and the Word of Man*, trans. D. Horton, (Gloucester, MA: Peter Smith, 1978).

Introduction

In the published version of my doctoral dissertation, *Covenanted Solidarity*, I sought to trace the development of Barth's views on election and revelation from Safenwil to Basel, as a way of entering into the theological basis of his radical theologico-political opposition to Nazi antisemitism. In this first book I suspended my journey in 1948. The last major historical event with which that project dealt, and this only very briefly, was Barth's 'take' on the creation of the State of Israel, in light of his understanding of divine providence and the Jewish recovery after the *Shoah*.

There was never any doubt, in my mind at least, that a vital part of the story had still to be told. Indeed, in the first substantive review of that book, by Duncan Forrester,[1] the questions that in his view had been left unresolved were precisely the questions that I had already known would need further treatment in a subsequent study. As I have suggested above, not the least of the questions that required greater exploration was the relationship of providence to the creation of Israel in 1948, and the extent to which, in Barth's mind, this relationship opened the door slightly to a return of natural theology.

More broadly is the place of Karl Barth in the post-Holocaust theological milieu. In *Covenanted Solidarity*, the historical emphasis of my study was to properly contextualize Barth's *Church Dogmatics* in the complex and inter-related environs of theological post-liberalism, social antisemitism, and the political influence of Nazism. In this present book, on the other hand, I have endeavoured to locate Barth in the context of post-Holocaust theological debates and the corresponding initiatives in Jewish–Christian dialogue. I am well aware that many of my fellow scholars would find it surprising that Barth could be placed within this context. Nonetheless, I am convinced that his contribution to the state of theology in the second-half of the twentieth century must take into account his role in responding to the most serious of crises by which at least Christian theology was challenged in this period. Contrary to others, I would argue that the *Shoah* was (and remains) a far greater problem for orthodox Christianity than the neo-liberalism of John Robinson, the so-called 'death of God' movement, or the challenge of feminist theology.

Kendall Soulen has cogently argued that one of the inevitable consequences of doing theology after Auschwitz is that the Church has had to question itself, not only about its relationship to the *people* of Israel, but indeed also about its relationship to the *God* of Israel. This God is, he says, 'the firm foundation and inescapable predicament of Christian theology.' As with many others, Soulen has recognized that, in a post-Holocaust age, it is impossible to do theology without reference to this God of Israel—but to pursue theology *with* reference to this God places Christianity in a

---

1   D. Forrester, Review of *Covenanted Solidarity*, in *IJST*, vol. 5, no.3 (2003).

'struggle for its very life.'[2] Why should this be the case? The supersessionist model, according to which the Church has replaced Israel in the economy of God, has been widely discredited in the last sixty years. On the other hand, it has been largely ignored that this repudiated doctrine 'is constitutive of the view of the economy that funds classical trinitarian theology...' In Soulen's view, the identity of the God of Israel as YHWH is, according to classical trinitarianism, 'finally dispensable for understanding God's *eternal* identity...'[3] Thus, to fully grapple with the problem of supersessionism means also to confront the question of the identity of the God whom Christianity proclaims—and, therefore, of course, to confront the identity of Christianity itself. In saying this, I do not wish to imply that Barth understood himself to be engaging consciously in this sort of post-Holocaust theology. Nonetheless, it is his theological contribution in relation to the debates stirred up by this movement with which this book is primarily concerned.

In choosing this as the book's central focus, I have deliberately had to raise the question of changes in Barth's post-war theology when compared to the themes with which he was busy during the 1930s–40s. Whereas some Barth scholars have assumed an internal uniformity within his dogmatics that precludes the possibility of fundamental changes in theological direction, I am rather more convinced that, within the context of overall consistency, Barth's mind nonetheless did change over time—as, in fact, a book of his reflections precisely indicates.[4] And so, it has seemed self-evident to me that one cannot presuppose that Barth's wartime views were the same as his later ideas.

There is, of course, a danger in polarizing theories of Barthian theology: those who read a consistency into his 57-odd years of theological activity need to take care not to overlook the variations in nuance that clearly occurred in Barth's thinking; similarly, those who see his theology as evolutionary should not and do not necessarily argue that there were no connecting threads. Having said this, however, I have come rather firmly to the opinion that Barth's pre-Göttingen theology was in substantial measure different to the views he began to explore and articulate in Bonn, and then later in Basel, but that the last of his cycles of dogmatics (the Bonn–Basel *Kirchliche Dogmatik*) did indeed exhibit greater internal uniformity. As has been said by others before, the *Church Dogmatics* are a vast exercise in saying much the same thing over and over again, from different perspectives.

On the other hand, however, I would be showing a false hand if I gave the impression that I see no continuity between Barth's theological content and method before and after Bonn, or that I see no measure of change in his so-called 'mature' dogmatics. The presence of dialectic right throughout the *Church Dogmatics*, so ably demonstrated by Michael Beintker and Bruce McCormack, is sufficient proof of the continuity that exists with his earlier *Romans* period. The nature of Barth's 'Israel theology' (if indeed he had such a thing) after the Holocaust is, I hope to show in

---

2   R.K. Soulen, *The God of Israel and Christian Theology*, (Minneapolis: Fortress Press, 1996), ix.

3   R.K. Soulen, 'YHWH the Triune God', in *Modern Theology*, vol.15, no.1 (1999), 25.

4   K. Barth, *How I Changed My Mind*, ed. J.D. Godsey, (Edinburgh: St Andrew Press, 1969).

this book, evidence that even in his late work he was not blind to new ideas. (I must add here that, while throughout the book I will use the terms 'Israel theology' and 'theology of Israel' to describe Barth's understanding of biblical and post-biblical Israel, I am far from convinced that he himself would have used the term. There is, in Barth's dogmatics, no doctrine or theology of Israel in and of itself. Rather, he insists that the question of Israel is to be seen in the context of broader themes such as election, revelation and, as we shall see, providence.)

I have been well aware that in exploring this assumption, I have had to challenge my own presuppositions. I have argued elsewhere that Barth's resistance to natural theology, so crucial to his stubborn opposition to Nazism and the *Deutsche Christen*, made it difficult for him to employ even the horrendous events of the Nazi era to inform his own theology. So, for example, I see no clear evidence that his exposition of radical evil (*das Nichtige*) in *CD* III/3 takes into account the rupturing effect of the Holocaust on all modern thought-forms, including Christian theology. This assumption is explored in detail in Chapter Three. And yet it is precisely the suspicion that the Holocaust informed Barth's post-war understanding of Israel that lies behind this book. Whereas I for one, have never accepted that Barth's theology was, either consciously or not, antisemitic, I do believe that the *Shoah* compelled him toward a more deeply empathetic attitude towards the Jewish people that was reflected in his last theological writings. Thus, nuanced variations, alongside overall consistency!

I should add a personal note here. My suggestion that Barth's opposition to natural theology hindered him from fully acknowledging the theological impact of the Holocaust does not mean that I necessarily think his opposition was in itself wrong. My own views on the legitimacy of natural theology remain conflicted, for as much as I hold the *Shoah* to be a modern theological datum, I am wary of extending this recognition to other events. It is an open question how and if such events could be so recognized, within what doctrinal paradigm, and by what criteria. I will explore this in some small detail at the close of Chapter Three. Suffice it to say here that, if push comes to shove, I would edge toward Barth, even while acknowledging the inconsistency in my own position. Thank goodness, then, that what I am trying to do in this book is explore Barth's views, and not trying to give precise formulation to my own!

In addition to the question of natural theology, there are certain issues integral to the structure of the *Church Dogmatics* with which this book deals that, I hope, set it apart from others in the field. Two of the most important books in recent years to explore Barth's relationship to Israel and the Jews have been Eberhard Busch's *Unter dem Bogen des einen Bundes*, and Katherine Sonderegger's *That Jesus Christ was Born a Jew: Karl Barth's 'Doctrine of Israel'*. It would be fair to say both books focus on slightly different aspects of the problem. Busch is concerned to explore the way in which Barth established the theological basis for why the German Church had to stand in solidarity with the Jews during the Nazi period and, as a result of that theological foundation, why it had also to stand politically against Hitler's antisemitic agenda.

Sonderegger, on the other hand, is far more scathing of Barth's perception of Israel, and regards his political activism on the Jews' behalf, and particularly on behalf of the Israeli State, more as a pleasant surprise than as something that could have been expected on the basis of this theology. She does acknowledge Barth's moral courage and ecclesiastical leadership during the Nazi era; nonetheless, she is concerned that his formulation of the doctrine of election perpetuates traditional anti-Judaic stereotypes. Ironically, in view of the age-old caricatures that it sustains, Barth's doctrine of election is the one 'genuinely new' theological development that he achieved. With election being the very basis of his *Israellehre*, Barth thus locates his theology of Israel 'at the heart of his most powerful and innovative...statement.'[5] Having said this, however, Sonderegger is determined to show why, in her view, Barth's theological 'take' on Israel is notably deficient for the task of post-Holocaust theology generally, and Jewish-Christian dialogue specifically.

To a certain extent, therefore, Busch and Sonderegger talk past each other. What both books show, however, is that Barth's 'theology of Israel' is far more nuanced than either his critics or his admirers have often assumed. Barth's recognition during the Holocaust years of the fundamental covenantal solidarity that exists between Jews and Christians should not blind us to his caricaturized image of the 'Synagogue', which makes Jewish–Christian dialogue problematic. Conversely, such deficiencies should not mask the moral and spiritual courage of his leadership during the dark days of Nazism.

Far more problematic in my view is the fact that neither Busch nor Sonderegger explore in any depth Barth's dogmatic attitude toward Jews and Judaism in what is surely the most central of all Christian doctrines, the doctrine of reconciliation. In December 1949, Barth said in a radio address that what divides Jews and Christians is also what binds them together, that is, 'the Jew on the cross on Golgotha.'[6] In this light, it seems to me imperative that Barth's understanding of Israel and the Jews be considered through the lens of *Church Dogmatics* IV. This consideration, in Chapter Five, forms the climax of this present book. It is my deep hope that in my exploration of this question, emphasis will fall on the positive side of the paradox of which Barth spoke, namely, that Jews and Christians might be more harmoniously *bound together*.

---

5   K. Sonderegger, *That Jesus Christ was Born a Jew: Karl Barth's 'Doctrine of Israel'*, (Pennsylvania State University Press, 1992), 45–46.

6   K. Barth, 'The Jewish Problem and the Christian Answer', in *Against the Stream: Shorter Post-War Writings, 1946–1952*, trans. E.M. Delacour & S. Godman, (London: SCM Press, 1954), 200–201.

Chapter One

Jewish–Christian Relations Since 1945

In the sixty-odd years that have passed since the end of the Second World War, possibly no subject has received more attention from scholars, artists, poets and novelists than the Nazis' war against the Jews. As long ago as 1980, George Kren and Leon Rappoport estimated that by the end of the twentieth century, more would have been written about the Holocaust than about any other subject in human history.[1] Having entered the twenty-first century, their claim may or may not now be sustainable. What is without dispute, though, is that the Holocaust, or *Shoah*, as it may be more appropriately termed,[2] has continued to generate enormous debate as people have endeavoured to comprehend its magnitude, its motivation, and its ramifications.

With the obvious exception of the many Jewish communities throughout the world, it is arguably the case that nowhere has the fallout from the *Shoah* been more acute than within Christian theology and, more particularly, in the relationship of the Church to the Jewish people. Admittedly, this is a contentious claim. Some modern German historians would argue that the impact of the Holocaust on European Jewry is mirrored only by Germany's collective post-war experience. A curious consequence of Daniel Goldhagen's 1996 study, for example, is that by 'restoring the perpetrators'—that is, the German people themselves—'to the center of our understanding of the Holocaust', Germany becomes the only nation capable of sharing with Jews an understanding of the magnitude of the Holocaust's effects.[3] Historians of some other countries that suffered under Nazi occupation could, however, make a similar point. Richard Lukas, for example, argues that the experiences of non-Jewish Poles 'provide a somber reminder that [they] were just as likely as Jews to suffer at the hands of the Nazis, who viewed them with nearly

---

1   G. Kren & L. Rappoport, *The Holocaust and the Crisis of Human Behavior*, (New York: Holmes & Meier, 1980), 1.

2   This is not the place to enter into a sustained discussion on the linguistic history of the word 'Holocaust', nor on its problematic usage when referring to the Nazis' war against the Jews. Suffice it to say here that, while 'Holocaust' continues to be the most commonly used term to describe Hitler's genocidal program, it is becoming less and less popular amongst scholars. *Shoah* (a Hebrew word meaning total destruction) and/or the Yiddish expression *Churban* (catastrophe) are increasingly being employed as more appropriate replacement terms. Throughout this book, I use Holocaust and *Shoah* interchangeably, aware on the one hand of the disturbingly sacrificial overtones inherent in the term Holocaust, but aware also that scholarship, let alone public usage, has yet to fully embrace its Hebrew alternatives.

3   D.J. Goldhagen, *Hitler's Willing Executioners: Ordinary Germans and the Holocaust*, (London: Little, Brown & Co., 1996), 6.

equal contempt.'[4] Poland, in fact, presents a most interesting case. With the *Aktion Reinhard* death camps of Bełżec, Sobibór and Treblinka, as well as Auschwitz-Birkenau, being located in Poland, it was long believed by Poles that the Holocaust was in fact a specifically *Polish* tragedy. This belief was compounded by the 'more than forty years of state-imposed ignorance', that disenfranchised the possibility of a uniquely Jewish experience.[5] It has only been in Poland's relatively recent past that such attitudes have begun to change.

These arguments against the Jewish specificity of the Holocaust have merit. On the other hand, Goldhagen's attempt to place the German people at the centre of Holocaust perpetration has hardly received general consensus. Similarly, the history of the relationship between German and/or Polish non-Jews to their Jewish countryfolk is both ambiguous and contentious. Periods and places of extreme antisemitism co-exist with periods and places of surprisingly harmonious interaction. In consequence, the ramifications of the Holocaust on German–Jewish and Polish–Jewish relations can only be understood if one accepts that, as destructive as it may at times have been, neither German nor Polish history as such conspired to make the Holocaust inevitable.

It is at this point, I believe, that one can legitimately argue that the impact of the *Shoah* has fallen more heavily upon Christianity than upon any other group or institution other than the Jewish people themselves. Unlike Germany or Poland, the pre-Holocaust history of the relationship between the Church and the Jews was anything but ambiguous. Rather, popular antisemitism throughout the generations was shored up by official antisemitism that routinely emanated from the various seats of Christian authority, from Rome to Luther. This history, so tainted by anti-Jewish vitriol, has meant that in the wake of the Holocaust the Church has been unable to avoid a confrontation with its past.

Franklin Littell, Alice and Roy Eckardt, and John Conway are just some of the many Christian scholars of the Holocaust who have articulated the dilemma.[6] In the same way that European—and especially German—Christianity, was wrenched by a crisis of credibility after the First World War, the Church and its theology have been decisively ruptured by the Holocaust that occurred during the Second World War. After centuries of contemptuous teaching about the Jews, including their (alleged) social malfeasance and rejection at the hand of God, the Church has been forced to reconsider and revise its age-old position. In the words of Richard Harries,

---

4 R.C. Lukas (ed.), *Forgotten Survivors: Polish Christians Remember the Nazi Occupation*, (Lawrence: University Press of Kansas, 2004), front-cover material.

5 C. Rittner & J.K. Roth, 'Memory Offended: The Auschwitz Convent Controversy', in F.H. Littell, A.L. Berger & H.G. Locke (eds), *What Have We Learned? Telling the Story and Teaching the Lessons of the Holocaust*, (Lewiston: The Edwin Mellen Press, 1993), 382.

6 See for example: F.H. Littell, *The Crucifixion of the Jews: The Failure of Christians to Understand the Jewish Experience*, (Macon: Mercer University Press, 1986), 2; A.L Eckardt & A.R. Eckardt, *Long Night's Journey Into Day: A Revised Retrospective on the Holocaust*, (Detroit: Wayne State University Press, 1988); J. Conway, 'Christianity and Resistance: The Role of the Churches in the German Resistance Movement', paper presented at the Birmingham conference on *Resistance and Christianity*, April 1995.

the *Shoah*, has quite properly, shocked the Christian churches into asking searching questions about its responsibility for what happened and about its historic relationship to Judaism.[7]

This necessary questioning has been, and continues to be, a long and at times tortuous journey, characterized by ambiguity and mutual mistrust as much as by genuinely harmonious and fruitful dialogue. Hannah Holtschneider has pointed out that there are three rough phases in the post-Holocaust history of Jewish–Christian relations. In the immediate aftermath of the Second World War, there was a general sense of shock, especially in relation to the evidence of the Holocaust, which rendered serious critical reflection almost impossible. As John Conway has observed, it was

> [not] until the middle 1950s, as the details of the crimes perpetrated against the Jewish people became more fully known, did Christians begin to realise that the events of the *Shoah* posed vital and inescapable questions about the complicity and culpability of the churches, not least concerning the sins of omission and lack of compassion and charity.[8]

From the 1960s through the 1980s, official encounters between Jews and Christians provided the impetus for the various Church pronouncements that repudiated both the Holocaust and the antisemitism on which it was based. Since the 1980s, confessional declarations have been largely replaced by the fruit of academic theological discussions.[9] Throughout these three phases, there have been many high-points of interaction, perhaps most notably the visit by Pope John Paul II to the Wailing Wall in Jerusalem in 2000. On the other hand, such progress as has been made has occasionally been undermined by insensitivities, such as the convent controversy at Auschwitz in the late 1980s, and the canonizations of Maximillian Kolbe (1981) and Edith Stein (1998).

Obstacles Along the Way

Father Maximillian Kolbe's canonization was, at one level, undeniably deserved. A Franciscan priest from Poland, he offered to take the place of Franciszek Gajowniczek, a fellow inmate in Auschwitz who was married with children but who had been selected for summary execution. Kolbe's offer was accepted by the camp commandant—a sacrificial death by which Gajowniczek was saved. On the other hand, Kolbe's attitude towards Jews was far less savoury. At best, he was a 'conversionist' (that is, he believed that Jews could only be saved if they renounced their Judaism and became Christians); in the opinion of others, he was 'rabidly anti-Semitic [*sic*].'

---

7   R. Harries, *After the Evil: Christianity and Judaism in the Shadow of the Holocaust*, (Oxford: Oxford University Press, 2003), 8.

8   J.S. Conway, 'The Changes in Recent Decades in the Churches' Doctrine and Practice Towards Judaism and the Jewish People', in *...und über Barmen hinaus. Studien zur Kirchlichen Zeitgeschichte*, (Göttingen: Vandenhoeck & Ruprecht, 1995), 537.

9   K.H. Holtschneider, *German Protestants Remember the Holocaust: Theology and the Construction of Collective Memory*, (Münster: LIT Verlag, 2001), 37.

Edith Stein's memory is similarly problematic. She was a Jewish philosopher from Breslau who converted to Catholicism in 1922, became a member of the Carmelite Order, and perished in Auschwitz in August 1942. Rachel Brenner has argued that Stein battled with the co-existence of two religious identities within herself. While her conversion was undoubtedly authentic, she 'remained loyal to her Jewish roots and publicly proclaimed her Jewish identity.'[10] In 1933, for example, Stein wrote that 'God ha[s] once more laid a heavy hand upon his people—my people.' Later, in her final testament which she wrote in 1939, she prayed 'for the Jewish people...for the deliverance of Germany and peace throughout the world...for all my relatives...may none of them be lost.'[11] Clearly, there was a degree of duality to Stein's identity. From the perspective of the Nazis, she was imprisoned and murdered because she was a Jew; from the perspective of the Catholic Church, she died as a Christian martyr. From a Jewish perspective, however, Stein's name evokes *both* the recollection of a heroic Jewish woman *and* a rejection of Judaism. It is little wonder, then, that both Kolbe and Stein, notwithstanding the impressive force of their personalities, provoke such deeply contradictory responses.[12]

Having said this, however, it is quite clear that in its decision to canonize Stein and Kolbe, the Vatican was well within its rights. While aspects of their lives were, and remain, sources of confusion and concern to Jews, both individuals also demonstrated undeniable courage, humanity and integrity of faith in the most nightmarish of circumstances. Moreover, both died in genuinely sacrificial fashion. To withhold appropriate acknowledgment from them would have been, in its own way, offensive to their memories.

The Carmelite convent controversy at Auschwitz was, on the other hand, a quite different matter, and one that was far more damaging to Catholic–Jewish relations. John Roth and Carol Rittner have said, indeed, that the controversy 'seriously jeopardized' the fruit of previous Catholic–Jewish dialogues.[13] Rubenstein has gone even further. According to him, the dispute

> brought to the surface many of the persistent wounds of the still unmastered trauma of World War II. Some of the most difficult aspects of Jewish–Christian and Jewish–Polish relations were once again made manifest...[The] situation had gotten so out of hand as needlessly to jeopardize the very real progress made in Jewish–Catholic relations since Vatican II.[14]

Rome may have had legitimate cause to canonize Kolbe and Stein, but with the proposal in 1984 to construct a convent in buildings immediately adjacent to

---

10 R.F. Brenner, 'Edith Stein, the Jew and the Christian: An Impossible Synthesis?', in Littell, Berger & Locke, 226.

11 W. Herbstrith, *Edith Stein: A Biography*, trans. B. Bonowitz, (San Francisco: Harper & Row, 1983), 64, 95. Cited in Brenner, 226.

12 See J.E. Young, *The Texture of Memory: Holocaust, Memorials and Meaning*, (New Haven: Yale University Press, 1993), 145.

13 Rittner & Roth, 'Memory Offended', 379.

14 R.L. Rubenstein, *After Auschwitz: History, Theology, and Contemporary Judaism*, (Baltimore: The Johns Hopkins University Press, 1992), 62.

Auschwitz-I, the Catholic Church stepped well outside the bounds of decency. The fact that the nuns' occupation of the buildings went ahead without any consultation with members of any Jewish community exacerbated Jewish feelings of betrayal and suspicion.

In its initial iteration, the aim of the Carmelite sisters who moved into the Old Theatre was simply to commit themselves to a life of prayer, in confession for the crimes committed at Auschwitz and in honour of the martyrs who had perished within its walls. In and of itself, this may not have caused significant offense, even if the building chosen for the site had at one time been used by the SS guards as a storehouse for Zyklon-B canisters, a fact which no doubt rendered it a less than salubrious venue. What provoked far greater, and entirely understandable, anger from Jewish groups was the move by a Belgian Catholic group in 1985 to turn the place of prayer into a 'spiritual fortress and guarantee of the conversion of strayed brothers…, as well as proof of our desire to erase outrages so often done to the Vicar of Christ [Pope Pius XII].'[15] Far from being a place of confession and of prayerful remembering of Auschwitz's dead, the convent was now to be the symbolic centre of a concerted effort to evangelize Jews, and to whitewash the history of Pius XII's ambivalence.

These are just two of the events which have pock-marked the road toward Jewish-Christian reconciliation since 1945. There are many other events which have, conversely, been sources of hopeful celebration rather than hostility and mistrust. It is within this ambiguous journey of reconciliation and dialogue that the work of Karl Barth must be seen. Never one to do his theology in a social vacuum, Barth found himself increasingly unable to separate his post-war theology from the questions with which the Church was inevitably confronted because of the war. While it would be disingenuous to suggest that Barth was a deliberate pioneer of interfaith theological dialogue in the same sense as people like Paul van Buren and Hans Küng, it would be equally incorrect to suggest that Barth was entirely ambivalent about the state of Jewish–Christian relations, or that he did not work hard to eliminate the anti-Jewish elements that had for so long contaminated the Church's teaching. Debate quite properly continues, therefore, over the exact role that can be attributed to Barth in the Church's post-Holocaust reorientation. Whereas the remainder of this book will focus attention on Barth's post-war theology itself insofar as it bears upon the question of Israel, this first chapter will survey the trends within post-Holocaust relations between Jews and Christians. In this way, Barth's role will stand out in hopefully sharper, and more accurate, relief.

Confessional *mea culpas*: Church statements addressing the Holocaust

It did not take long for Germany's Protestant Churches to begin their reflections on the period of Nazi rule. As early as August 1945, leaders of the Evangelical Church met in Treysa to discuss their response to the restructuring of post-war Germany. Karl Barth and Martin Niemoeller took the lead as they had done during the *Kirchenkampf*, and

---

15 Young, 146.

urged the necessity not simply of ecclesiastical restoration but indeed of repentance. Similarly, Hans Asmussen called upon the Church to acknowledge its guilt first, and only then to embark upon the task of restructuring itself.

> How we wish that we knew nothing of all this and could start anew. But the world grants us no rest: she screams to us with questions of guilt, and whether we will or not, we must answer. We must answer our own nation and we must answer the whole world.[16]

When the Churches' leadership met again in Stuttgart in October, they did indeed confess that, during the years of Nazi rule, they were guilty of 'not witnessing more courageously, [of] not praying more faithfully, [of] not believing more joyously and [of] not loving more ardently.'[17] This confession, as important as it was, nonetheless hid deep divisions amongst the churchmen. For some, notably Bishop Wurm, the Stuttgart Declaration went too far in its confession of guilt. That such divisions existed meant that, on the contrary, the Declaration was entirely unable to go far enough. In the same way that Germany's Churches, even the *Bekennende Kirche*, opposed various Nazi policies but never the regime itself, the Stuttgart Declaration was equally selective in the guilt that was in fact acknowledged; as Conway reminds us, it said nothing about 'the worst atrocity of all, the extermination of the Jews.'[18] The Holocaust was widely regarded as a specifically Jewish tragedy, the blame for which lay with secular not Christian forces.[19]

Two years later at Seeligsberg in Switzerland, Jewish and Christian leaders met under the banner of the International Council of Christians and Jews. The driving-force behind this gathering was the French scholar Jules Isaac. The resultant 'Ten Points of Seeligsberg' included a forceful denunciation of the 'noxious doctrine of Jewish responsibility for the Crucifixion' and a recognition that the notion of perpetual Jewish reprobation was a baseless superstition.[20] This document was no doubt significant. Its major drawback, however, was that it did not have the endorsement of any of the major Christian denominations, and thus it had no institutional authority. Rather, the 'Ten Points' were largely the product of concerned individuals—both Christian and Jewish—who had already been active in the area of interfaith dialogue for some time.

The necessity and timeliness of the Stuttgart and Seeligsberg statements notwithstanding, it is clear that neither went as far as desirable, nor did they have the authority that one would ideally have wished or that was desperately needed. In any case, these two statements aside, the relationship between Jews and Christians in the immediate aftermath of the Second Word War was, as we have already noted, characterized by a shocked silence. Perhaps the wounds were too raw. As Alice Eckardt has suggested, the initial ecclesiastical responses to the *Shoah* took the form

---

16 H. Asmussen, cited in J.S. Conway, 'How Shall the Nations Repent? The Stuttgart Declaration of Guilt, October 1945 ', in *Journal of Ecclesiastical History*, vol.38, no.4 (1987), 617.

17 Conway, 'How Shall the Nations Repent?', 596.

18 Conway, 'How Shall the Nations Repent?', 620.

19 Conway, 'The Changes in Recent Decades in the Churches' Doctrine', 537–538.

20 Conway, 'The Changes in Recent Decades in the Churches' Doctrine', 541.

of 'a slow but difficult awakening, as though God were enticing the churches onto untried paths.'[21] Whatever the reason, it was not until 1965 that the most significant step in Jewish–Christian dialogue was taken.

Nostre Aetate

A full twenty years after the downfall of the Third Reich, the Roman Catholic Church—for nearly two millennia the authoritative seed-bed of Christian antisemitism—pioneered a new direction for Christian thinking about Israel, and proved that centuries of suspicion and animosity could be overcome by the force of *teshuva* and goodwill. It was, in fact, remarkable that Rome should have taken such a lead. The Catholic reaction to the Holocaust throughout the late 1940s and through almost the entire 1950s was marked by silence. Only among a handful of theologians, such as John Öesterreicher, Karl Thieme and Gregory Baum, was there any attempt to grapple with the theological and ethical failures of the Roman Catholic Church during the Nazi years. When the change came, it coincided with the death of the conservative Pius XII in October 1958 and the election of Angelo Roncalli, who took the name John XXIII, as his successor, one month later.

From the first, Roncalli demonstrated that he would be 'a powerful and dynamic personality.'[22] Not only did he create the first (black) African and the first Japanese cardinals, he also signaled his determination to deal with Catholic–Jewish relations. In 1959, the new pope—who in September 2000 was recommended by the International Raoul Wallenberg Foundation for recognition by Yad Vashem as a 'Righteous Gentile'—took the bold move to delete from the Good Friday liturgy the prayer *pro perfidis Judaeis*. Three years later, and after an enormous amount of preparatory work, John XXIII solemnized the opening of the Second Vatican Council. By the end of the Council in 1965, many of the most destructive of Christianity's historic teachings about the Jews were, through the watershed document *Nostre Aetate*, decisively repudiated.

Nostre Aetate—perhaps, because it dealt with the relationship of the Catholic Church to those outside its boundaries, the single most important document to emerge from Vatican II—was not exclusively concerned with Catholic–Jewish dialogue. In seeking more open interaction with all religions, the document made clear that 'the Catholic Church rejects nothing of what is true and holy in these religions', even admitting that such religions 'often reflect a ray of that truth which enlightens all people.' Forty years on, we can be tempted to see in these statements only a patronizing superiority. In Michael Wyschogrod's wonderfully insightful comment, 'in [*Nostre Aetate*], the non-Christian religions are spoken *about*, not spoken *to*.'[23] We should not, however, underestimate the enormously progressive nature of *Nostre*

---

21 A.L. Eckardt, 'How are the Protestant Churches Responding 50+ Years After?', in J.K. Roth & E. Maxwell (eds), *Remembering for the Future: The Holocaust in an Age of Genocide*, (Basingstoke: Palgrave, 2001), vol.2, 533.

22 P. Lapide, *The Last Three Popes and the Jews*, (London: Souvenir Press, 1967), 309.

23 M. Wyschogrod, 'Israel, the Church and Election', in J. Öesterreicher (ed.), *Brothers in Hope*, (New York: Herder & Herder, 1970), 79.

Aetate. According to Shalom Ben-Chorin, Vatican II was no less than a 'Copernican shift' in the relationship of Catholicism to Jews and Judaism.[24] Rabbi David Rosen has gone even further, calling *Nostre Aetate* 'one of the greatest revolutions in human history.'[25] On the fortieth anniversary of *Nostre Aetate*, another Jewish scholar, Rabbi Anson Laytner, described it as 'the tentative embrace that marked the beginning of...reconciliation.'[26] Moreover, while the document did discuss other religions, its principal focus was indeed Catholic–Jewish relations.

Among its more important declarations, *Nostre Aetate* excised from official Church teaching the notion that Jews are, by default, rejected or accursed on account of the death of Christ. 'Neither all Jews indiscriminately at that time, nor Jews today, can be charged with the crimes committed during [Jesus'] passion.' Furthermore, instead of seeking to lay blame on a particular perpetrator, *Nostre Aetate* preferred to find the cause of Jesus' death in the fact that 'out of infinite love [he] freely underwent suffering and death...' This is not to say that Rome repudiated its own supersessionist agenda; 'the Church is the new people of God...' Nonetheless, the myth of automatic reprobation for all Jews, and the murderously dangerous charge of deicide, were forcefully denounced. By any standard, these changes to official Catholic teachings were momentous. More than that, they 'must now be taken as *normative teachings* of the Church...'[27]

Of particular interest here is Barth's response to Vatican II. He held Pope John XXIII in especially high esteem, regarding him as a genuine *pastor bonus*. At last, thought Barth, in this pope 'we have seen one who has at least shown some quite definite characteristics of the good shepherd.'[28] Even after John XXIII's death, Barth followed Vatican II assiduously, and was in fact invited by Cardinal Bea to attend the third session of the Council. Due to poor health, he had to decline. Hans Küng, however, kept Barth fully informed of all that was happening—in itself, a sign that Barth followed the Council's progress with great interest. In September 1966, Cardinal Bea repeated his invitation to Barth. This time, Barth was able to accept, and he spent a remarkable six days in Rome, holding both open and confidential conversations with Bea, Rahner, Ratzinger and, to conclude, with Pope Paul VI. It is hardly surprising, then, that he could write that, 'I took an increasing interest in the results of the Second Vatican Council...' [*CD* IV/4, viii]. Indeed, Barth 'made a serious study of the sixteen Latin texts produced by the Council and of at least some of the abundant literature devoted to [it].'[29] It seems implausible that *Nostre Aetate*

---

24 Shalom Ben-Chorin, *Israel Nachrichten*, 6 December 1991.

25 D. Rosen, cited in R. Modras, 'Addressing the Demonic in Sacred Texts: Catholic–Jewish Relations After the Holocaust', in Roth & Maxwell, vol.2, 442.

26 A. Laytner, at the 'Vatican II; Nostre Aetate, 40 Years and Into the Future Symposium', 19 October 2005, Seattle University.

27 Conway, 'The Changes in Recent Decades in the Churches' Doctrine', 545. My emphasis.

28 K. Barth, conversations with students at Tübingen, 2 March 1964. Cited in E. Busch, *Karl Barth: His Life from Letters and Autobiographical Texts*, trans. J. Bowden, (Grand Rapids: Eerdmans, 1994), 467.

29 K. Barth, *Ad limina apostolorum*, (Zürich: Evangelischer Verlag, 1967), 10. Cited in Busch, *Karl Barth*, 481.

was not one of the texts which aroused Barth's interest, particularly in light of his comment in 1966 to the Vatican Secretariat for Christian Unity: 'There is', he said, 'finally only one really great ecumenical question: our relations with the Jewish people.'[30] Rome apparently agreed; despite its shortcomings, *Nostre Aetate* was the first major demonstration after the Holocaust that Roman Catholicism at least was seeking to address this great ecumenical question. In the words of Edward Flannery, *Nostre Aetate* 'terminated in a stroke a millennial teaching of contempt of Jews and Judaism and unequivocally asserted the Church's debt to its Jewish heritage.'[31]

In 1974, the Vatican presented a follow-up document to *Nostre Aetate*, rather awkwardly entitled *Notes on the Correct Way to Present Jews and Judaism in Preaching and Catechesis of the Roman Catholic Church*. In spite of its cumbersome title, this document has proven invaluable in creating a new paradigm of Catholic hermeneutics. It recognized, for example, that

> it cannot be ruled out that some references hostile or less than favourable to the Jews have their historical context in conflicts between the ancient church and the Jewish community. Certain controversies reflect Christian–Jewish relations long after the time of Jesus.[32]

By being prepared to contextualize the various antisemitic texts within the New Testament, the Vatican was, through this document, showing its willingness to 'read against' the Scriptures. Such an approach has, in the years since these *Notes* were published, 'set out practical ways in which this new relationship with Judaism could be fostered by correct teaching...As a result of this some impact has been made on individual Roman Catholic priests, teachers, and congregations.'[33] As Edward Kessler has rightly said,

> in a very short space of time (the last 40 years), the Roman Catholic Church has produced a remarkable series of documents, which have not only repudiated its anti-Jewish theology but have reversed it. The Jewish people are no longer viewed as cursed but blessed.[34]

The 1980 Rhineland Synod

It took a further fifteen years for Protestant Churches to follow the lead of their Catholic brethren. While it may be the case now that 'most churches of the West have been responding to [the *Shoah*] one way or another...', it took quite some time for this momentum to be gather pace.[35] It was not until 1980 that the first major

---

30 Harries, 99.

31 E. Flannery, 'Seminaries, Classrooms, Pulpits, Streets: Where we have to go', in R. Brooks (ed.), *Unanswered Questions: Theological Views of Jewish–Catholic Relations*, (Notre Dame: University of Notre Dame Press, 1988), 128–129.

32 See E. Fisher, *Catholic–Jewish Relations; Documents from the Holy See*, (Washington, DC: Catholic Truth Society, 1999), 43.

33 Harries, 231.

34 E. Kessler, 'The Jewish People and their Sacred Scriptures in the Christian Bible: A Response to the Pontifical Biblical Commission Document.' See www.jcrelations.net (2003).

35 Eckardt, 'How are the Protestant Churches Responding?', 533. Eckardt also rightly acknowledges that some Churches, such as the Uniting Church of Australia, 'are only beginning'

advance was made, when the Evangelical Church in the Rhineland published the statement, 'Towards a renewal of the relationship between Christians and Jews.' Holtschneider notes that the Rhineland Synod was

> the first of the member churches of the EKD [*Evangelische Kirche im Deutschland*] to declare the relationship of Christians and Jews…to be of fundamental importance for the self-understanding and well-being of the Christian church.[36]

This is not to suggest that the statement emerged from a vacuum. Since 1965 the Rhineland Synod had been actively exploring Jewish–Christian relations, and had even established a Study Commission for the Relation of the Church to Judaism. Nonetheless, the 1980 synodical statement was a *novum* for the EKD. In Holtschneider's words, it 'symbolise[d] [*sic*] a new dimension of theological work.'[37] John Conway, similarly, has commended the Rhineland statement for 'expressly referr[ing] to the Holocaust as the crucial factor necessitating the attainment of a new relationship between the church and the Jewish people.'[38]

However, its positive contribution to post-Holocaust theological reflection notwithstanding, the statement does suffer from some conspicuous flaws. There is, for example, an evident unwillingness to view the Holocaust from a Jewish perspective. Perhaps this is understandable, and even appropriate, given the identity of the statement's authors. It would surely be cause for controversy had the Synod attempted to speak 'as though' it was speaking with a Jewish persona. On the other hand, there is a somewhat more problematic result of the Synod's failure to identify with Jewish perspectives. In a manner similar to historians such as Richard Lukas, whose work has already been noted above, the statement argues that Jews were not the only victims of the Holocaust. Rather, it claims that the Holocaust should be understood chiefly in the context of a crisis of civilization and culture, with Christians in Germany being 'no less affected than Jews by [its] consequences…'[39] Clearly, there is a need to acknowledge that Christianity as such *has* been forever challenged by the *Shoah*, and the Synod's statement is right to make this acknowledgment. But, on purely quantitative terms, it is demonstrably impossible to equate the existential identity-crisis faced by Christianity with the murder of six million Jewish people, and to suggest such an equation ('no less affected…') is little short of blasphemy.

Holtschneider is also critical of the Rhineland Synod for instrumentalizing Jews. The statement's intent 'is to show the continuing salvation-historical significance of the Jewish people' and, insofar as that is the aim, the Synod is to be applauded. There is, at the very least, an attempt to repudiate the age-old replacement theology by which Jews were understood to no longer have any share in God's work of salvation in the world. Given that replacement theology was foundational to the view, firstly, that the Jews no longer had any right to eternal life and then, by logical extension under Nazism, that they no longer had any right to life itself, the Rhineland Synod's

---

to deal with the theological consequences of the Holocaust to their theology. See p.533.
  36 Holtschneider, 39.
  37 Holtschneider, 40.
  38 Conway, 'The Changes in Recent Decades in the Churches' Doctrine', 539.
  39 Holtschneider, 45.

attempt to counter this theology deserves credit. Holtschneider believes, however, that in re-claiming a positive significance of Jews in God's design, the Synod has ignored the many competing paradigms of Jewish identity that have emerged among Jewish communities in the wake of the Holocaust. Instead of listening to how Jews now define themselves, the Synod has instead sought to force back into theology a conception of Jewish identity that is now anachronistic and unrepresentative of contemporary Jewish understanding.[40]

Holtschneider has rightly identified areas of concern within the Rhineland Synod's 1980 statement. However, the positive dialogical intent of the statement should not be forgotten even as its shortcomings are acknowledged. As Allan Brockway has noted, the statement is, in most important aspects, 'extremely sensitive to the theological nuances of Christianity vis-a-vis Judaism…'[41] As a stepping-stone toward greater mutual understanding between these two religions, the document was of vital significance.

In the same year as the Rhineland Synod of the EKD published its groundbreaking document, the Baden Provincial Synod took a similarly strong stance. 'In conformity with biblical teaching' it was necessary for Christians to establish a new way of relating to the Jewish people, that fully acknowledged 'the inseparable link between the New and Old Testament', and the ongoing covenantal relationship of Israel to God.[42]

Across the Atlantic, the Presbyterian Church, in both 1982 and 1987, unequivocally stated its commitment to the 'irrevocable' election of both Jews and Christians, while the United Methodist Church affirmed that God continues 'to work through Judaism and the Jewish people.'[43] These positive moves were, it has to be admitted, somewhat undermined by the ambiguous position that both Churches continued to endorse regarding the evangelization of the Jews. Neither could bring themselves to accept that the conversion of Jews to Christianity was redundant for Jewish salvation. Less problematic was the declaration of the United Church of Christ in 1987, in which it was stated with remarkable forthrightness that 'Judaism has not been superseded by Christianity; that Christianity is not to be understood as the successor religion to Judaism; [and that] God's covenant with the Jewish people has not been abrogated.'[44] Ten years later, the United Church of Canada similarly rejected the theological legitimacy of evangelistic missions to the Jews, with the Evangelical Church of Austria following suit in 1998.

Such statements and declarations from Churches and various synodical bodies have been of immeasurable value, even when one takes into account their shortcomings. At the very least, the right questions are being asked and there is a

---

40 Holtschneider, 51–59.

41 A. Brockway, 'The Theology of the Churches and the Jewish People', Centre for the Study of Judaism and Jewish–Christian Relations, Birmingham, 1989.

42 H. Croner (ed.), *More Stepping Stones to Jewish–Christian Relations*, (New York: Stimulus Books/Paulist Press, 1985), 161.

43 Eckardt, 'How Are the Protestant Churches Responding?', 536.

44 See Eckardt, 'How Are the Protestant Churches Responding?', 536–537. Other Churches to reject the theological legitimacy of missions to the Jews include the Evangelical Church of Austria and the United Church of Canada.

clear *intent* to arrive at the correct answers. The statements are not, however, the only way in which both Catholic and Protestant Churches have been responding. Possibly more significant than the public statements—necessary as they undoubtedly are— have been the attempts by various Churches to modify their liturgy. We have already noted the Catholic repudiation of the Good Friday prayer. Among Protestants, other similarly notable changes have been accomplished.

A very early attempt to construct an appropriate post-Holocaust liturgy was produced in 1972 by Elizabeth Wright, and was celebrated in the chapel of Queen's College in Charlotte, North Carolina. Among the many strengths of this 'Yom HaShoah Liturgy for Christians' are its employment of contemporary Jewish voices—for example Wiesel, Schwarz-Bart, Nelly Sachs and Chaim Kaplan—and its deliberate confession of Christian culpability in the *Shoah*. On the other hand, the liturgy makes explicit reference to the cultic significance of the word 'holocaust', and grants legitimacy to the sacrificial overtones of the word even when used to refer to the murder of the Jews.[45]

More recently, the British Columbia Conference of the United Church of Canada has urged that care be taken when using lectionary readings with antisemitic overtones. Going even further, the national governing body of the United Church of Canada issued specific instructions in 1997 regarding the use of antisemitic texts within the Gospels.

As with the official synodical and denominational statements of confession and repentance, none of these liturgical modifications is or has been sufficient in isolation. Moreover, in each case it is possible to highlight faults and shortcomings. This is probably inevitable inasmuch as the Churches will and should continue to speak as *Christian* Churches; they can hardly be faulted for wanting to stay true to their religious heritage. But progress is being made, and there is an ever-increasing recognition of the need for hermeneutical and liturgical sensitivity.

Conclusion

To sum up this first chapter, therefore, it is important to acknowledge that the path toward Jewish–Christian reconciliation over the past sixty or so years has been marked by both successes and controversies. After the initial years of shock, during which the world community began to realize the full magnitude of the *Shoah* and also, therefore, the enormity of its failure to stop it, there has been slow but generally steady progress made amongst the Churches in confronting the legacy of Christian antisemitism. From the Protestant side, the 1980 statement from the Rhineland Synod of the EKD was the first official declaration that took seriously the impact of the Holocaust on Christian theology. Fifteen years earlier, *Nostre Aetate* had led the Catholic Church to much the same conclusion. This, indeed, was and remains probably the high-water mark of Jewish–Christian relations since 1945.

Over the past ten years, further progress has been made. Again, it is notable that Rome has led the way. In 1998, Pope John Paul II gave his unequivocal endorsement

---

45 'A *Yom HaShoah* Liturgy for Christians', in Littell, 141–153.

to the document 'We Remember: A Reflection on the *Shoah*'. Though beset by some significant deficiencies, not least of all the refusal to accept institutional culpability for the so-called 'teaching of contempt', 'We Remember' was at least commended by numerous Jewish commentators for its tone and intent. According to Yehuda Bauer, 'the document has to be evaluated positively', while Britain's Chief Rabbi, Jonathan Sacks, regarded it as 'a step forward'. Michael Berenbaum, too, while accepting that 'Jews didn't get everything they wanted,' was convinced that 'what they got was so significant.'[46]

'We Remember' was followed up by John Paul II's remarkable visit to Jerusalem in 2000 during which he stopped to pray at the Wailing Wall. In the same year, the National Jewish Scholars' Project, based in Baltimore, issued 'Dabru Emet'(lit. 'speak the truth'). This statement was an attempt to recognize and celebrate the 'dramatic and unprecedented shift in Jewish and Christian relations', and to affirm the many points of contact between the two faiths.

As this chapter has shown, not every interaction between Christians and Jews has been so positive. However, it is happily evident that the overwhelming ecclesial trend is toward greater awareness of and sensitivity to the Church's Jewish heritage. More importantly, this awareness is increasingly being defined by a recognition that the legacy is not purely historical; that in fact the Church has (and must have) a continuing relationship, not only with post-*biblical* Judaism, but indeed also with post-Holocaust Israel.

It is within this overall context of post-war interfaith dialogue that we must locate Karl Barth. Barth did not, of course, live to see all the progress in Jewish–Christian relations that has been described here. He did, however, experience at close hand, and comment upon, the Stuttgart Conference, the establishment of Israel in 1948, and the publication of *Nostre Aetate*. He cannot, therefore, be ignored when one considers the span of Jewish–Christian relations since 1945, and so it is within the context painted here that the remainder of this book must be understood.

---

46 See K. Madigan, 'A Survey of Jewish Reaction to the Vatican Statement on the Holocaust', in Roth & Maxwell, vol.2, 428.

Chapter Two

Barth and the Jewish People: The historical debate

In Chapter One, we surveyed the history of Jewish–Christian relations since 1945. It was apparent there that the nature of this history has been punctuated by as many extraordinary highs as by devastating lows. For anyone who has worked in the fields of Barth, Holocaust and/or *Kirchenkampf* studies, it would come as no surprise that the nature of the relationship between Karl Barth and the Jewish people has also been hotly contested for some time. For those for whom these areas of study are somewhat newer, however, it may indeed not be so self-evident why this should be the case. For some, the assumption that all Christian theology is deeply anti-Judaic, or perhaps even antisemitic,[1] would logically entail a certain hostility between Barth and the Jews. Indeed, it could be thought—and has certainly been argued—that Barth's consistent Christocentrism makes his theology so much more susceptible to an at least implicit and subconscious anti-Jewishness. Others, taking the opposite view, might regard a Judaeo-Christian covenantal bond as a theological given, and therefore assume a natural affinity between the two. Still others will come to the question on the (false) presupposition that a uniform relationship existed between Nazism and the German Churches that, again, entailed a particular stance, either positively or negatively, on Barth's part. While the truth is significantly more complex than any of these individual preconceptions suggest, they do nonetheless help explain precisely why the nature of Barth's relationship with (both biblical and post-biblical) Israel remains so fiercely controversial.

Wolfgang Gerlach, R. Kendall Soulen and, to a lesser extent, Katherine Sonderegger characterize the argument that there is an inherent antisemitism deeply embedded within Christianity from which Barth, try though he may, could not escape. Daniel Jonah Goldhagen makes the same point, but in harsher and theologically ill-considered language. Robert Ericksen and Richard Gutteridge exemplify those who regard Barth's position as essentially neutral, on the two-fold assumption of a general ecclesiastical attitude that was by default conservative and right-wing, and of which Barth was himself an inheritor, as well as by virtue of Barth's own 'transcendentalized' theology. The difficulty with such neutrality, argue this group of

---

1   I make the distinction between anti-Judaism and antisemitism because, although the former was the necessary precondition for the Nazis' version of the latter, I nonetheless believe that there remains a qualitative difference between the two. Further, in what follows I deliberately use the term 'antisemitism' *without* a hyphen, except where direct quotations insist otherwise. I make this choice simply because, when spelled with a hyphen, the term implies the validity of the racial category 'Semite'.

scholars, is that during times of crisis (such as the German *Kirchenkampf*), Church leaders were and are impotent to provide ethical leadership. Indeed, neutrality within crisis almost inevitably segues into passive endorsement. If Barth did take an essentially neutral line, he would thus be guilty of the most wilful neglect of Nazism's victims—he would, in other words, be that most dangerous of people, 'the bystander' who, in doing nothing, allows evil to flourish.

Eberhard Busch and I, although hopefully neither out of theological nor historical shortsightedness, represent a smaller number of scholars who have endeavoured to show that it was Barth's own *theology*—rather than an instinctual empathy (which, in fact, he did not recognize in himself)—that enabled him to adopt a pro-Jewish political stance, both during and after the Holocaust. The intent of this chapter is to flesh out these various positions, and so provide a context in which the remainder of the book's arguments can be read and assessed.

The Context of Controversy

Karl Barth, 'the most important Protestant theologian since Schleiermacher'[2], certainly also one of the greatest Christian theologians from any confession since the Reformation—and perhaps even since Aquinas, according to Pius XII—is nonetheless also one of the most controversial and least understood. Barth himself seems to have recognized this when, in the foreword to Weber's digest to the *Church Dogmatics*, he lamented the fact that he existed 'in the phantasy of far too many…only in the form of certain, for the most part, hoary, summations…'[3] George Hunsinger is therefore quite correct when he notes that, partly due to the 'labyrinthine argument' of his theology, especially as proposed within the *Church Dogmatics*, Barth may be widely honoured but he is rarely read. To get a feel for precisely how problematic any interpretation of Barth's theology is, it is worth quoting Hunsinger at some length.

> Barth is so deeply traditional and so strikingly innovative, so rigorous in argument and so daring in conception, so simple in essence and so complex in development, so narrowly focused and so wide-ranging in scope, so passionate in commitment and so relentless in criticism, so exasperating in disagreement and so inspiring in devotion, that nothing would be more welcome than a single conception to unlock the whole…[H]owever, such a conception is unlikely to be found.[4]

No more clearly is this the case than in his understanding (I hesitate to call it a 'doctrine') of Israel and contemporary Judaism. Both his personal relationships with Jews and his theological perspective on Jews and Judaism are ambiguous and problematic. Barth's obituary in *The Times* may have said that 'he continued to champion the cause of the Confessing Church [and] the Jews…', but this eulogizing

---

2   J. Webster, *Karl Barth*, (London: Continuum, 2004), 1.

3   K. Barth, 'Foreword to the English Edition', in O. Weber, *Church Dogmatics: A Selection*, (London: Lutterworth Press, 1953), 7.

4   G. Hunsinger, *How to Read Karl Barth: The Shape of His Theology*, (New York: Oxford University Press, 1991), 3, 27.

has hardly met with universal acceptance.[5] As Paul van Buren has said, 'Barth really understood *Torah* as good news to Israel [but only poorly understood] that *Torah*-living by the Jewish people was living by grace.'[6] If, therefore, it was claimed above that both during and after the Holocaust Barth was politically pro-Jewish—or at least, vehemently opposed to political antisemitism—this must be qualified by the recognition that his theological language often betrays an ignorance of the Judaism of his day.

In the same way that the legacies of Bultmann, Heidegger and Kittel have all been tainted to a greater or lesser degree by their (real and perceived) associations with Nazism, so too has Barth's theological legacy—with its complex and ambiguous understanding of Israel—been subjected to intense scrutiny in the post-Holocaust age.[7] No moderate acquaintance of his with individual Jews and/or their religious writings has been enough to shelter him (and nor should it) from criticism. As both Christian and Jewish theologians have argued, the Holocaust poses the greatest challenge to the ongoing validity of individual theologies. The late Emil Fackenheim spoke of the Holocaust as a 'decisive rupture' in all modern *Denkforms*, while Dietrich Ritschl has said that it is no longer possible to do theology after Auschwitz 'to the exclusion of this fundamental wound.'[8] Inevitably, then, the theological agenda of even—and indeed especially—the 'greatest theologian since Aquinas' have come under scrutiny and in the process generated enormous debate. Moreover, the intricate complexities of Barth's theology itself, which themselves cause so much confusion amongst commentators, simply serve to add another level of controversy to what would have been in any case an analytical and inter-religious minefield.

---

5   *The Times*, 11 December 1968, 10.

6   P. van Buren, 'Probing the Jewish-Christian Reality', in *Christian Century*, (June, 1981), 665–668.

7   The German phenomenologist Martin Heidegger (1889–1976) joined the NSDAP in 1933 and was a vocal and public supporter of the National Socialist government during his tenure as Rector of the University of Freiburg. Gerhard Kittel (1888–1948) was (and still is) one of the most respected Lutheran scholars of the New Testament, but was also a member of the Nazi Party and of the *Deutsche Christen*. Rudolf Bultmann (1884-1976) should not, of course, be listed alongside Heidegger and Kittel, as he was a member of the Confessing Church and an opponent of the Nazi regime. Nonetheless, Bultmann's theological method caused Barth to fear that he would align himself with the German Christian Movement. As he wrote to Bultmann on 10 July 1934: 'Do not be upset anymore that I was in fact filled with distrust to the extent that I had expected to see you turn up among the *DC*. It has been proved by the facts that I made a mistake in this case…You must grant me only the general truth that it was possible to suspect anyone of anything this crazy year but also the particular truth that you did not make it easy for me to see clearly in advance that you would not do what Heidegger had done with drums and trumpets and also Gogarten, whom I had to regard as the normative theologian in your eyes. According to my observations it was a fact that all those who worked positively with a natural theology or the like *could* become *DC* and that most of them…*did* so.' See B. Jaspert (ed.), *Karl Barth–Rudolf Bultmann Letters, 1922–1966*, (Edinburgh: T & T Clark, 1982), 76.

8   E. Fackenheim, *To Mend the World: Foundations of Post-Holocaust Jewish Thought*, (New York; Shocken Books, 1989), *passim*; D. Ritschl, *The Logic of Theology*, (London: SCM Press, 1986), 128.

It is also important to realize in this context that the parameters of Holocaust scholarship have changed in recent years. Whereas the first generation of scholars— Yehuda Bauer, Lucy Dawidowicz, Raul Hilberg and company—trawled the archives for quantitative and instrumental data that would build up the picture of the 'How, When, Where and How Many', the focus has now changed to more evaluative questions. In other words, now that the basic empirical issues have generally speaking been resolved (and, with the exception of the revisionist fringe, broadly accepted), attention has shifted to the lessons that can and must be learned from the Holocaust. Michael Marrus puts it this way:'so long as our intellectual life is free and challenging, new questions will rain down on Holocaust history. Count on the next generation to frame different problems even for the sources we have already examined.'[9] Thus, post-Holocaust theology and the inherent challenges that it poses for traditional Western Christian doctrine has become as vital a scholarly discipline as history or politics.[10] The gravity and polemic associated with the debates over Barth's 'Israel theology' can be understood only in this context.

With all this in mind, what in fact are the various divergent views of Barth's personal, theological and political relationships to Jews and Judaism? I will defer the question of politics—specifically as it relates to Barth and the State of Israel—to Chapter Four. Barth's attitudes on this topic can in any case only be appreciated on the basis of his theology. Consequently Chapter Three will consider Barth's attitude toward natural theology, as it confronted him in the immediate aftermath of the Second World War, and the extent to which the Holocaust caused him to re-think his rejection of it. Chapter Four will extend this discussion by looking at Barth's theological and (on this basis) political response to the creation of Israel in 1948. To what extent was Barth's response to the Israeli State influenced by his understanding of the *Shoah* and, if it was in some measure influenced by it, does this signal a concession to natural theology? Finally in Chapter Five, we will give in-depth consideration to Barth's theological understanding of 'the Jews' as put forward in *CD* IV, 'The Doctrine of Reconciliation', both in terms of the consistency of his theology of Israel and the extent of its evolution in the light of Nazism, the Holocaust and Israel's declaration of independence. The remainder of this chapter will provide the context in which the questions of the later chapters must be asked. To this end, we need to look first at what we know of Barth's personal relationship with Jewish people, and how his attitude towards Jews and Judaism has been variously assessed by other scholars.

---

9   M.R. Marrus, 'The Holocaust: where we are, where we need to go—a comment', in M. Berenbaum & A.J. Peck (eds), *The Holocaust and History: the known, the unknown, the disputed, and the re-examined*, (Bloomington: Indiana University Press, 2002), 33–34.

10 It is worth noting that the legacy of the Holocaust is most deeply felt by Western Christianity, specifically in Europe and North America. To say this is not to suggest that its legacy is only relevant to Western Christianity, but simply to acknowledge that, for a variety of reasons, the Holocaust has not had a uniform impact across the globe. Jewish–Christian dialogue remains in its infancy, for example, within Eastern (Orthodox) communities, and even in some Western countries such as Australia, the Churches have only just begun to address the theological challenges of the *Shoah*.

Reading Barth's Ambiguity

Arguably the single biggest challenge to Barth scholarship is the sheer volume of his work. Even discounting his thirteen half-volumes of (unfinished!) *Church Dogmatics*, his output was remarkable. The internal 'insights and vistas' of Barth's theology itself add another layer of complexity to the interpretive task, as does his peculiarly individualistic manner of structuring his thoughts. As Webster and others have noted, Barth writes his *Dogmatics* as though he were writing a symphony.

> No one stage of the argument is definitive...Barth's views on any given topic cannot be comprehended in a single statement...but only in the interplay of a range of articulations.[11]

Little wonder, then, that commentators and scholars have found it so difficult to adequately categorize him as one sort of theologian or another. Was he, as commentators as far apart as John McConnachie and George Hunsinger have suggested, a 'theologian of the Word'?[12] Was he, alternatively, a 'dialectical theologian', as he has most commonly been described? Others have latched on to a dominant theme in his earliest published works and have tried to box him as a 'theologian of Crisis', even though the crisis of which he spoke in the aftermath of the First World War was radically different to the all-pervading sense of shock that beset the rest of Europe, including its intellectual life. Perhaps Barth can best be described as 'neo-orthodox'—or even, as Bruce McCormack's doctoral dissertation suggested, a type of 'neo-Scholastic'?[13] More recently, McCormack has challenged the entire analytical paradigm that has driven Barth scholarship since Von Balthasar's 1951 textbook *Karl Barth: Darstellung und Deutung Seiner Theologie*, by discarding the dialectical–analogical periodization that was normatively read into Barth's early writings.

Such arguments over the interpretation of Barth's theology apply in the first place to Barth's theological method. Equally, however, the content of his theology has been the topic of strenuous debate. Cornelis Van Til and Stanley Hauerwas, to take just two examples, reflect the polarities. A little over sixty years ago Cornelius Van Til, a particularly scathing critic, asked rhetorically, 'Has Karl Barth Become Orthodox?', only to answer (entirely predictably) that he had not.[14]

> It is, we believe, to do Barth injustice, and to do the church irreparable harm, when orthodox theologians fail to make plain that dialectical theology is basically subversive

---

11 Webster, 13–14.

12 J. McConnachie, *The Significance of Karl Barth*, (London: Hodder & Stoughton, 1931), 93*ff*; G. Hunsinger, *Disruptive Grace: Studies in the Theology of Karl Barth*, (Grand Rapids: Eerdmans, 2000), 48. See also H.U. von Balthasar, *Karl Barth: Darstellung und Deutung Seiner Theologie*, (Köln: Jakob Hegner, 1951); ET *The Theology of Karl Barth*, trans. E.T. Oakes, S.J., (San Francisco: Ignatius Press, 1992), 28.

13 B.L. McCormack, *A Scholastic of a Higher Order: The Development of Karl Barth's Theology, 1921–1931*, (Princeton: Princeton Theological Seminary, 1989).

14 C. Van Til, *Has Karl Barth Become Orthodox?*, (Philadelphia: The Presbyterian and Reformed Publishing Company, 1954).

of the gospel of saving grace…No heresy that appeared at [Nicaea, Chalcedon, Dort or Westminster] was so deeply and ultimately destructive of the gospel as is the theology of Barth.[15]

Barth and his entire system is, says Van Til, anathema to 'historic Christianity.'[16] Conversely, Stanley Hauerwas, arguably the foremost theologian from the Anabaptist tradition throughout the past century, takes Barth to be the greatest authentic witness to the Word of God in the modern age, the one who 'reclaim[ed] the scriptural and theological resources of the Christian tradition…'[17]

Perhaps, then, one of Barth's first commentators had it right: that it is impossible to fit Barth into any known theological scheme because to almost every scheme he is a *scandalon*.[18] Moreover, his theology moves and never crystallizes. As Hugh Mackintosh realized early, Barth 'offers clear principles, definite assumptions, but never a closed system. [It is] theology on the wing…'[19] In Barth's own words (albeit in a different context), it is 'a most precarious attempt to imitate the flight of a bird' [*Rom* II, 184]. Or, as Dietrich Bonhoeffer suggested to a seminar group at Union Theological Seminary in 1931, 'I do not see any other possible way for you to get into real contact with Barth's thinking than by forgetting everything you have learnt before.'[20] Indeed, to cite Bonhoeffer at this point is particularly apt. Steven Haynes has recently noted that Bonhoeffer's theological legacy has been appropriated by everyone from the liberal and liberation theologians to those on the far-right of conservative evangelicalism; his person and his work are so richly nuanced that he can, rather regrettably, be press-ganged into supporting almost any theological position.[21] The same is perhaps not quite so true of Barth, but it is clear that he resists being easily categorized and, as a result, has been both claimed and demonized by the entire range of theologies.

It is not just in relation to his theology, however, that Barth has proved so hard to pigeon-hole. His personal relations—be they with his wife Nelly, his secretary Charlotte von Kirschbaum, Emil Brunner, Bonhoeffer, or in the context of this present study particularly his relations with Jews and Judaism—have also resisted easy definition. One writer has in fact overtly singled out this ambiguity by referring to Barth's alleged antisemitism being hidden behind the 'amicable guise of

---

15 Van Til, *Has Karl Barth Become Orthodox?*, 181.

16 C. Van Til, *The New Modernism: An Appraisal of the Theology of Barth and Brunner*, (London: James Clarke & Co, 1946), 366.

17 S. Hauerwas, *With the Grain of the Universe: The Church's Witness and Natural Theology*, (London: SCM Press, 2002), 240 and *passim*.

18 McConnachie, 242.

19 H.R. Mackintosh, *Types of Modern Theology: From Schleiermacher to Barth*, (London: Nisbet & Co., 1937), 264.

20 *GS* III, 111.

21 S.R. Haynes, *The Bonhoeffer Phenomenon: Portraits of a Protestant Saint*, (Minneapolis: Augsburg Fortress, 2004).

philo-semitism'.[22] In this context of competing interpretations, is it possible to reach a more definitive understanding? It is to this question that we now turn.

Barth and the Jewish People: How scholars have understood him

There is no doubt that the majority of theological and historical scholars who have concerned themselves with the question of Barth's attitude toward the Jewish people have concluded that he was at best ambivalent and, at worst, openly hostile toward them. Very few scholars have tried to argue that Barth was racially antisemitic; even his harshest critics recognize the qualitative differences between Nazi-style racial ideology and the anti-Jewishness they see in Barth. However, his condemnation of politico-racial antisemitism notwithstanding, it is argued that when it came to engaging with real people, Barth could not overcome a profoundly visceral antipathy toward individual Jews. The controversial Catholic theologian, Hans Küng, whose own work on Judaism has received critical acclaim from Jews and Christians alike, is in the minority when he says that 'it took [Barth's] *Church Dogmatics*...to open my eyes...at least to the explosiveness of the theme and the undeniable dialectic of synagogue and church.'[23]

Most scholars, however, disagree with Küng's grateful acknowledgment of Barth's perceptiveness. Often without fully examining his dogmatic theological writings, Barth's critics routinely cite two pieces of apparent evidence for this attitude, both of which were personal letters by Barth to fellow-theologians that date from the last years of his life. They are worth considering in some detail.

The first is the letter sent by Barth to Eberhard Bethge in 1967 on the publication of Bethge's biography of Bonhoeffer. In that letter, Barth acknowledged Bonhoeffer's leadership in the struggle against Nazi antisemitism, confessing that 'I have long since regarded it as a fault on my part that I did not make this question a decisive issue...'[24] His interests, he admits, were elsewhere—specifically, with preparing the ground for and then authoring the Barmen Declaration. Indeed it is regrettably true that, although there was a condemnation of National Socialist ideological hubris,

---

22 H. Jansen, 'Antisemitism in the Amicable Guise of Philo-Semitism in Karl Barth's Theology Before and After Auschwitz', in *Remembering for the Future: Papers Presented at the International Scholars' Conference*, (Pergamon Press, 1988), 74. For other studies on Barth's personal relations and their impact upon his theology, see: S. Selinger, *Charlotte von Kirschbaum and Karl Barth: A Study in Biography and the History of Theology* (University Park, PA: Pennsylvania State University Press, 1998); E. Röhr (ed.), *Ich bin was ich bin: Frauen neben großen Theologen und Religionsphilosophen des 20. Jahrhunderts*. Originalausg. (Gütersloh: Gütersloher Verlagshaus, 1997); A. Pangritz, *Karl Barth in the Theology of Dietrich Bonhoeffer*, (Grand Rapids: Eerdmans, 2001).

23 H. Küng, 'My Encounters with Judaism', in R. Walter (ed.), *Das Judentum lebt—ich bin ihm begegnet. Erfahrungen von Christen*, (Freiburg im Breisgau, 1985), 121. Cited in K.-J. Kuschel & H. Häring (eds), *Hans Küng: New Horizons for Faith and Thought*, (New York: Continuum, 1993), 258.

24 Letter, Barth to Bethge, 22 May 1967. *Letters, 1961–1968*, ed. J. Fangmeier & H. Stoevesandt, trans. G.W. Bromiley, (Edinburgh: T & T Clark, 1981), 250.

the Declaration itself said nothing explicitly about the Jewish persecution. On the other hand, however much the Declaration was a product of Barth's own hand it was, nonetheless, intended as a public statement from the wider Confessing Church. In this light, it is instructive to note that in the same letter to Bethge, Barth contends that a specific reference to Nazi antisemitism, had it been included by him, would in any case not have garnered support from the other Confessors. His hindsight, while not an excuse, is probably accurate, if one considers the unambiguously non-political history of the *Bekennende Kirche* after Barmen.

But what of Barth himself? Does Barmen's silence on the question of the Jewish persecution mirror Barth's own stance? Irrespective of Barmen's failure to unequivocally condemn antisemitism, a strong case can be mounted to argue that in his confession to Bethge, Barth is in fact being unduly harsh on himself. By early September 1933, for example, as soon as the Prussian General Synod had forcibly passed the Aryan Paragraph, Barth recognized that the Church was in *status confessionis*. In other words, at precisely the same time that Bonhoeffer—who is usually regarded as having been the first Church leader in Germany to have arrived at this conclusion—pronounced that the Church was in *status confessionis*, Barth also came to that realization. Just a few days prior to the General Synod, Barth had written to Frau Dalmann, saying that

> The Jewish question is surely…the symbol of all events of our time. Precisely in [this issue] could I not take the smallest step with National Socialism. I believe that here, if anywhere, one must hear the command to halt, and see the border over which one can step only as a betrayal of the gospel…[25]

And again, in January 1934, in the wake of his controversial Advent sermon in which he explicitly wished to say 'a word *for* the Jews',[26] Barth wrote to a congregant in Bonn that 'anyone who believes in Christ, who was himself a Jew…*simply cannot* be involved in the contempt for Jews and ill-treatment of them which is now the order of the day.'[27] Barth's confession to Bethge of his disinterest in the suffering of the Jews during the early years of Nazism seems, therefore, to be a self-indictment that is not entirely consistent with the historical record. Nonetheless, the tendency has been for commentators to take Barth's words in 1967 at face value.

As further evidence that Barth's confession to Bethge may not in truth accord with the historic reality is the fact that Barth's 1933 pamphlet, *Theologische Existenz heute!* was not, in the end, the manifesto he wished to publish. In this pamphlet, in which he argued against the attempted 'coordination' (*Gleichschaltung*) of the

---

25 Letter, Barth to Frau Dalmann, 1 September 1933. Cited in E. Busch, *Unter dem Bogen des einen Bundes: Karl Barth und die Juden 1933–1945*, (Neukirchen-Vluyn: Neukirchener Verlag, 1996). 49. Curiously, and seemingly against all the evidence, Hans-Walter Krumwiede cites this letter as evidence of Barth's disinterest in the Jewish plight. See H.-W. Krumwiede, 'Göttinger Theologie im Hitler-Staat', in *Jahrbuch der Gesellschaft für niedersächsiche Kirchengeschichte*, 85 (1987), 160.

26 Sermon on Rom.15:5–13. Delivered by Barth in the Bonn *Schloßkirche*, 10 December 1933.

27 Letter, Barth to E. Steffens, 10 January 1934. Cited in Busch, *Karl Barth*, 235.

Church by the Nazi State and its idolatrous ideology, Barth spoke passionately in defense of Jewish Christians who were being forced out of congregational life by the imposition of racist legislation. Klaus Scholder has condemned Barth for omitting, in this manifesto as much as in the Barmen Declaration, the plight of Jews per se, arguing that his silence was 'deliberate'.[28] In fact, however, the pamphlet as it was published was, in Barth's own mind, fatally compromised. An earlier draft, which had been 'quite political, unprecedentedly sharp', had been softened by Barth on the stern advice of Helmut Traub and Charlotte von Kirschbaum, both of whom feared that the original version could prove dangerous. The end result—the version which in the end was printed—was angrily condemned by Barth: '*There's* your co-ordinated theological existence!'[29] Shortly afterwards, Barth complained to Thurneysen that 'I could have said a great deal more, but I had to button my lips a bit, so that I could just say that.'[30]

The second argument in support of Barth's alleged negative view of 'real' Jews once again comes from a letter written by him late in his life. Writing to Friedrich-Wilhelm Marquardt in September 1967, Barth notes that 'in personal encounters with living Jews…I have always, so long as I can remember, had to suppress a totally irrational aversion.'[31] In his defense, he immediately proceeds to acknowledge that this 'allergic reaction' is 'reprehensible'—nonetheless, the damage is done. In truth, this confession to Marquardt is far more damning than the letter to Bethge, and cannot be mitigated simply by recourse to history, to what Barth did or did not do for Jews during the Nazi years. By his own admission, Barth has forfeited the right to claim any philosemitic moral superiority. As Wyschogrod quite rightly says, such an honest admission makes it difficult to know what to do with Barth. 'One does not know whether to admire the man's courage for making the admission or to hold him in contempt for having the prejudice.'[32]

The response of most commentators to these admissions has, quite naturally, been to accept uncritically Barth's self-reflections. Moreover, his confession of an aversion to Jews with whom he had personal interaction has been read back into his theology. George Casalis, for example, who in so many ways is an admirer of Barth and who was himself active in aiding persecuted Jews, 'wonders whether [his treatment of the Jews in *CD* II/2] represents a description of any actual Jew, and whether the notion of "Israel" in that section has not become an abstract theological concept rather than the description of a living, flesh-and-blood group of real people.'[33] In similar language, John Bowden also expresses concern at Barth's abstraction of human suffering. He writes that

---

28 K. Scholder, *The Churches and the Third Reich*, vol.1, trans. J. Bowden, (London: SCM Press, 1987), 439.

29 H. Gollwitzer, 'The Kingdom of God and Socialism in the Theology of Karl Barth', in G. Hunsinger (ed.), *Karl Barth and Radical Politics*, (Philadelphia: Westminster Press, 1976), 113.

30 Letter, Barth to Thurneysen, 27 June 1933, in Busch, *Karl Barth*, 226.

31 Letter, Barth to Marquardt, 5 September 1967. *Letters 1961–1968*, 262.

32 M. Wyschogrod, 'A Jewish Perspective on Karl Barth', in D.K. McKim (ed.), *How Karl Barth Changed My Mind*, (Grand Rapids: Eerdmans, 1986), 160.

33 G. Casalis, *A Portrait of Karl Barth*, (New York: Doubleday & Co., 1964), xli.

One longs for him to say, just once, 'In the name of mankind, this is wicked,' for him to show insight into what other men, women and children feel and suffer as human beings. But this he cannot do.[34]

That Bowden makes this comment in the context of critiquing Barth's ethical passivity against Nazi racial persecution allows for no other conclusion than that Bowden finds Barth's attitude towards Jewish suffering fundamentally and inexcusably flawed.

The Jewish theologian, Michael Wyschogrod, has also leveled an accusation of antisemitism against Barth. Wyschogrod readily acknowledges that Barth, perhaps more than any other Christian theologian of modern times, is deeply impressive to the Jewish reader. Why this should be so is primarily due to Barth's humility before the divine word and his theological emphasis on God's movement toward humanity (*von oben nach unten*), as opposed to the 'Titanism' of liberal Protestantism by which humanity deems itself capable of reaching up to God (*Eritus sicut Deus!*). Nevertheless, in spite of this 'Jewishness' of Barth's theological method, the truth 'is that Barth's position towards Jews is ambivalent...[Barth suffers from] the traditional anti-semitism [*sic*] of European Christendom...and the anti-semitism [*sic*] of Christian theology.'[35]

While the criticisms leveled by Casalis, Bowden and Wyschogrod are undeniably harsh, it is vitally important to note that they come from commentators who are deeply and gladly indebted to Barth.[36] Their particular concerns, and indeed the extent to which they are legitimate, will occupy us in later chapters. There have, on the other hand, been a somewhat greater number of scholars whose accusations of antisemitism against Barth have been made from their own perspectives, not of indebtedness, but of grave suspicion toward him. In particularly strong language, Frank Talmage has argued that on the issue of the Jews, 'the thinking of a Christian anti-nazi [i.e. Barth] and that of a Christian nazi are not very far apart.'[37] Given

---

34 J. Bowden, *Karl Barth*, (London: SCM Press, 1971), 74–75.

35 M. Wyschogrod, 'Why Was and Is the Theology of Karl Barth of Interest to a Jewish Theologian?', in H.M. Rumscheidt (ed.), *Footnotes to a Theology: The Karl Barth Colloquium of 1972*, (Corporation for the Publication of Academic Studies in Religion in Canada, 1974), 107.

36 For other examples of appreciative but nonetheless critical assessments, see D.E. Demson, 'Israel as the Paradigm of Divine Judgment: An examination of a theme in the theology of Karl Barth', in *Journal of Ecumenical Studies*, (Fall, 1989), 611–627. Also, R.E. Willis, 'Bonhoeffer and Barth on Jewish Suffering: reflections on the relationship between theology and moral responsibility', in *Journal of Ecumenical Studies*, (Fall, 1987). Demson argues that Barth's exegesis of Rom.9–11 is both 'extensive' and 'profound', and yet at least linguistically requires recasting, so as to be rid of terminology that is no longer acceptable post-Auschwitz. Willis acknowledges the practical assistance given by Barth to Jews during the Nazi era, but nonetheless argues that his theological paradigm produces an 'eternal antisemitism' (p.614).

37 F.E. Talmage (ed.), *Disputation and Dialogue: Readings in the Christian–Jewish Encounter*, (New York: Ktav Publishing, 1975), 38. John Reid recognizes Talmage's accusation as a 'terrible misunderstanding', but also acknowledges that Barth's terminology of 'witness' contributes significantly to the misunderstanding. See J. Reid, 'Israel—People, Nation, State', in D.W. Torrance (ed.), *The Witness of the Jews to God*, (Edinburgh: The Handsel Press, 1982), 57*n14*.

Barth's uncompromising leadership of the Confessing Church's fight against the *Deutsche Christen Bewegung* (German Christian Movement), Talmage's accusation is impossible to sustain and in truth is little more than historical and theological nonsense. In more recent years, Daniel Goldhagen has passed an equally unsustainable verdict, at which he has arrived by reading isolated sentences of the *Dogmatics* and of sermons out of context. 'Karl Barth, the great theologian…was also an antisemite', whose personal animosity toward the Jews was 'deep-seated.'[38] As we have seen, Michael Wyschogrod also charges Barth with antisemitism. Where Goldhagen and Wyschogrod differ is in their respective interpretations of Barth's intent. For Wyschogrod, Barth's antisemitism is something against which he openly fights.

> To see Barth struggling toward the sign that is Israel, to see him fighting against his Gentile nature that demands antipathy to the people of election, to see this nature yield to the Word of God and to Barth's love for that Jew whom he loves above all others, is to see the miraculous work of God.[39]

Thus, when Wyschogrod charges Barth with antisemitism, it is from the perspective of warm appreciation for Barth's antipathy to the antisemitism which he saw in himself. When, on the other hand, Goldhagen levels the same accusation, it is with the intent of aligning Barth with all other representatives of 'eliminationist antisemitism', from John Chrysostom and Martin Luther, to Heinrich von Treitschke and Otto Dibelius.

Other scholars have similarly dismissed Barth. Either, he is regarded as someone whose focus upon a transcendentalized theology limited his ability to empathize with the sufferers of persecution (Richard Gutteridge). Or, as the evident leader of the *Bekennende Kirche*, he is judged to be highly culpable for the Confessors' reluctance to adopt a political stance against the Nazi State and its genocidal program (Pinchas Lapide).[40] By naive omission, an insistence on an anti-ethical theology, or even a willing adherence to the legacy of Christian antisemitism, Barth's otherwise brilliant theological work is thus irrevocably tainted by what, at face value, can only appear to be his suspicion of and visceral antipathy toward the Jews. This, at any rate, has been the common consensus of Barth's critics—amongst both theologians and historians, and also amongst both those who are sympathetic inheritors of his teaching, and those whose criticisms are more severe. The theological and political legitimacy of these assumptions will be tested in later chapters. The question for the remainder of this chapter will be whether Barth's personal interactions with individual Jews confirm these criticisms, or alternatively offer a portrait of Barth in which Jews figure more positively.

---

38 Goldhagen, 113.

39 Wyschogrod,'Why Was and Is the Theology of Karl Barth of Interest…?', 109.

40 R. Gutteridge, *Open Thy Mouth for the Dumb! The German Evangelical Church and the Jews, 1879–1950*, (Oxford: Basil Blackwell, 1976); P. Lapide, 'No Balm in—Barmen? A Jewish Debit Account', in *The Ecumenical Review*, vol.36, (October, 1984).

Barth and the Jews: His personal relationships

Many of the accusations of antisemitism that have been made against Barth rely upon the assumption that Barth's knowledge of Jews was entirely academic and based upon theoretical abstractions. As Busch words it, Barth's Christomonism was the reason that, in the eyes of many commentators, he was 'hindered...from seeing the Jews as concrete people.'[41] Emil Fackenheim, who is highly critical of Barth's emphasis on the 'triumph of grace' over evil, writes that 'Barth made *a few* attempts to speak to Jews toward the end of his life—*when...it was too late*.'[42] Katherine Sonderegger similarly notes that Barth was entirely ignorant of the actual substance of modern Jewish thought and of Judaism itself. He took no interest in familiarizing himself with the reality of Jewish religion. Indeed, his rejection of rabbinic Judaism was on the basis, not of Judaism's self-definition, but rather of his own assessment of it in the light of Scripture. In other words, a Judaism entirely unknown to the Bible is rejected by Barth on the basis of the Bible.[43] As Sonderegger has argued, Barth associates 'present-day Jews and Judaism' with the Second Temple Judaism of Pauline theology. However, she insists,

> we cannot make this association so quickly or directly. For the Judaism we know, and Jews themselves practice, is postbiblical or rabbinic Judaism; it is Judaism without the 'temple worship.'[44]

Perhaps most scathing in this regard has been Friedrich-Wilhelm Marquardt. In his view, Jews existed in Barth's mind as 'mere forms of our perception and the stuff of our alienated consciousness', having no independent reality.[45] In all three cases, Barth is assumed to have had no genuine encounters with Jewish people, at least not until late in his life, through which his doctrinal analysis of Israel, Jews and Judaism could have been humanized. To borrow a phrase from Eberhard Busch, however, these criticisms arise from 'a web of misinterpretations.'[46] Barth's theology was not simply abstracted from a predetermined theological paradigm. As we shall see, individual Jews were entirely real to him.

The Jews with whom Barth came into earliest contact were not only real to him but were highly influential as well. In 1908, Barth was finally given permission from his father to study at Marburg. The teacher to whom he was most drawn, and who in fact was the very reason for Barth wanting to go to Marburg in the first place, was Wilhelm Herrmann. As a dogmatician and ethicist, Herrmann was to have a decisive

---

41 E. Busch, 'Indissoluble Unity: Barth's Position on the Jews During the Hitler Era', in G. Hunsinger (ed.), *For the Sake of the World: Karl Barth and the Future of Ecclesial Theology*, (Grand Rapids: Eerdmans, 2004), 54.

42 Fackenheim, *To Mend the World*, 284. Emphasis added.

43 Sonderegger, *That Jesus Christ Was Born a Jew*, 3; Sonderegger, 'Response to "Indissoluble Unity" ', in Hunsinger, *For the Sake of the World*, 83–86.

44 Sonderegger, 'Response to "Indissoluble Unity" ', 82.

45 F.-W. Marquardt, *Die Entdeckung des Judentums für die christliche Theologie: Israel im Denken Karl Barths*, (Munich: Christian Kaiser Verlag, 1967), 316ff.

46 Busch, 'Indissoluble Unity', 55.

influence on Barth's theological education. However, as both McCormack and Fisher have admirably shown, Barth was not the student of an un-mediated Herrmann. Just as influential was neo-Kantianism, embodied in Marburg by the Jewish philosopher Hermann Cohen, and with which Marburg—and Herrmann—were thoroughly infused.[47] Barth was greatly impressed by Cohen. Later in his *Ethics*, Barth in fact cites Cohen in support of his repudiation of Germany's increasing racism, stating instead that 'the stranger within thy gates' is indeed also our neighbour.[48] In view of his later opposition to Nazi antisemitism, it is interesting to see that even in 1928, Barth was using his former Jewish teacher to bolster his theological denunciation of racism. While it would be disingenuous to suggest that Barth's enthusiasm for Cohen was due to his Jewishness, or even that Barth learned from him anything approximating orthodox Judaism, it is nonetheless clear that even in his student years Barth keenly sought out, and was heavily influenced by, Jews with whom he felt at least an intellectual affinity.

Once he was in the pastorate, Barth's opportunities for academic engagement were few and far between. Safenwil was a small industrial town in the Aargau countryside, and he very quickly learnt that an 'intellectual' pastor—who even tried to introduce his congregation to Hermann Cohen!—was neither understood nor wanted. Nonetheless, his final years in Safenwil opened up occasions for contact with individual Jews and Jewish Christians at both social and academic levels. Many of these were Germans, with whom Barth struck up friendships following the Tambach lecture of September 1919. Most notably, he came to know Hans and Rudolf Ehrenberg, Eugen Rosenstock-Hüssy and the great German Jewish philosopher Franz Rosenzweig, who together made up the so-called Patmos Circle. This eclectic but eminent group of philosophers, theologians and scientists was convinced—in the aftermath of the First World War—that civilization could be saved only by the daily spiritual and practical renewal of the Logos, embodied in speech and action. Not surprisingly, they drew both their name and their inspiration from John the Apostle, the 'Seer of Patmos'.

Barth was never really a member of the circle, but his association with the group seems to have lasted at least until the time of the founding of Patmos Verlag.[49] Indeed his Tambach lecture, 'Der Christ in der Gesellschaft', which had initiated Barth's association with the group in the first place, was printed as Patmos Verlag's very first publication.[50] While he sought later to distance himself from them (he believed that the spirit of the group was essentially gnostic), Busch does note that

---

47 See McCormack, *Karl Barth's Critically Realistic Dialectical Theology: Its Genesis and Development*, 1909–1936, (Oxford: Clarendon Press, 1995, repr.1997); S. Fisher, *Revelatory Positivism: Barth's Earliest Theology and the Marburg School*, (Oxford: Oxford University Press, 1988).

48 H. Cohen, *Ethik des Reinen Willens*, (Berlin, 1904), 382, in K. Barth, *Ethics*, trans G.W. Bromiley, (Edinburgh: T & T Clark, 1981), 195.

49 Freya von Moltke, Eugen's second partner and widow of the anti-Nazi conspirator Helmut von Moltke, even lists Barth as a fellow-founder of the publishing house. See 'Eugen Rosenstock Hüssy: A Brief Biography', The Norwich Centre.

50 See K. Kupisch, *Karl Barth in Selbstzeugnissen und Bildokumenten*, (Hamburg: Rowohlt, 1971), 45.

he regarded them, at least for a time, as 'friends'.[51] After the war, Barth could say of this association that they were 'positive relationships' and that, if they taught him anything, it was that 'God has a great variety of lodgers.'[52]

Barth's personal interaction with Franz Rosenzweig was not close—in fact, there is no definite evidence that the two ever actually met, despite Rosenzweig's heavy influence on the Patmos group. Nonetheless, Rosenzweig may well have been an intellectual influence on Barth. We know from Barth's correspondence with Kornelis Heiko Miskotte that in 1928 (at Miskotte's suggestion) he read Rosenzweig's *Der Stern der Erlösung*. It was clearly a hard book for Barth to understand (!), but it seems to have resonated with him. Specifically, Barth's use of terminology in *CD* II/2 strongly suggests that he concurred with Rosenzweig's vision of both the Church's evangelical role, and of the fundamental unity of God's community as expressed in Israel and the Church.[53]

It appears likely, then, that Barth was engaging with the works of leading Jewish theologians and philosophers of the day. But it is equally important to note that the exchange was reciprocal. In his *Ich und Du*, for example, Martin Buber writes that 'God is the "wholly Other"; but He is also the wholly Same, the wholly Present. Of course He is the *Mysterium Tremendum* that appears and overthrows; but He is also the mystery of the self-evident, nearer to me than my *I*.'[54] Maurice Friedman sees in this a qualified agreement with Barth's *Romans* theology; on the one hand endorsing Barth's emphasis on the 'Godness' of God, but on the other hand not losing sight of what Barth would (much) later come to refer to as 'the humanity of God.' It may be that Buber's reference to God as Wholly Other owes more to Søren Kierkegaard than to Barth, but the timing of *Ich und Du* (1923) in relation to the appearance of Barth's two *Romans* (1919, 1922) suggests that he was at least aware of, if not in some measure responding to, Barth's commentary.[55]

Further examples of the reciprocity of engagement between Barth and contemporary Jewish theologians come from the time of Barth's teaching career

---

51 Busch, *Karl Barth*, 112–113.

52 Letter, Barth to Heinrich Scholz, 2 August 1954; Letter, Barth to Thurneysen, in *Briefwechsel Karl Barth–Eduard Thurneysen, 1913–1921*, (Zürich: Evangelischer Verlag, 1973), 441.

53 See H. Stoevesandt (ed.), *Karl Barth–K.H. Miskotte: Briefwechsel 1924–1968*, (Zürich: TVZ, 1991), 79, 104. Also, Busch, 'Indissoluble Unity', 67–68. Also, F. Rosenzweig, *The Star of Redemption*, trans W.W. Hallo, (London: Routledge & Kegan Paul, 1971), 341*ff.*

54 M. Buber, *I and Thou*, trans R.G. Smith, (New York: Charles Scribner's Sons, 1954), 79.

55 M. Friedman, *Encounter on the Narrow Ridge: A Life of Martin Buber*, (New York: Paragon House, 1993), 343. In his foreword to the second English version of *Ich und Du*, Ronald Gregor Smith comments intriguingly that there were 'intricate connexions' (*sic*) between Buber and Barth that could not be confined to 'talk of any mere "influence"…in a simple way.' He goes on to note that 'Buber's own *Nachwort* to the volume, *Schriften über das dialogische Prinzip*…has a highly interesting comment on Barth's position as expressed in his *Kirchliche Dogmatik*, in the second part of the "Doctrine of Creation." To this might be added the remarkable recent essay by Barth, *Die Menschlichkeit Gottes*…' See R.G. Smith, 'Preface' in Buber, vi. Clearly, Smith perceives there to have been a deep and perceptive engagement by Barth and Buber in each other's respective works.

in Germany. In 1934 when Barth was Professor of Systematic Theology in Bonn, Berlin's pro-Zionist Rabbi Emil Cohn sent a copy of his *Judentum, ein Aufruf der Zeit* for Barth to read. While Barth was busy with Cohn's book, Barth's own writings were being read 'with lively attentiveness' within Cohn's Berlin synagogue.[56] But Barth's interaction with Cohn was not simply at a literary or theological level. In late February of the same year, Barth remarked to Cohn that, 'as a Christian [he] could only think with shame and terror [*Scham und Entsetzen*]' about what Jews in Germany were having to endure.[57] Clearly, their conversation touched upon the political realities of Nazi Germany as much as upon their respective theological endeavours. The very next year, Leo Baeck approvingly cited Barth's reference to Matthias Grünewald's Isenheim altar-piece, in which John the Baptist is shown pointing to Jesus on the cross. In Barth's Aarau lecture of 1920, he suggested that John's 'impossibly pointing' hand is the hand 'which is in evidence in the Bible.'[58] Baeck took up Barth's image to agree with him that 'the movement of this hand is the characteristic of Jewish existence.'[59]

In 1936, Barth was again engaged in dialogue with Martin Buber, through the initiative of Karl Ludwig Schmidt, editor of *Theologische Blätter*. In 1932, Buber had started work on the book that, four years later, was to be published as *Die Frage an den Einzelnen*. In a strikingly similar vein to Bonhoeffer's radio address of 1 February 1933, 'Der Führer und der Einzelne in der jungen Generation', Buber sought to distinguish between the genuine person of faith who believes within a community of faith, and the person who 'believes in' a leader (*Führer*). But he did not stop there. Just as crucially, Buber used the book to challenge the whole notion of collectivism, particularly as espoused by Gogarten. Within this context, Buber went on to repudiate Gogarten's affirmation of the radical and irredeemable evil of humanity. Schmidt's response to Buber's critique was to encourage Buber to seek out Barth's views on the notion of radical evil, which Buber indeed did. The reply from Barth showed clearly that both men were in substantial agreement as to, on the one hand, humanity's evil (sin) *coram Deo*, but on the other hand, the nonetheless still applicable command to love one's neighbour.[60] What is of most interest here is not so much the extent to which Barth and Buber were in agreement against Gogarten, but rather that Buber was interested in seeking out Barth's opinion as someone whose opinion Buber clearly valued.

Aside from the possible influence on Barth of Rosenzweig, there is no suggestion that Barth was especially enamoured with his Jewish dialogue partners of the 1920s and early 1930s. However, the charge that he was unfamiliar with modern Judaism and contemporary Jewish philosophy is clearly problematized by these connections

---

56 Busch, 'Indissoluble Unity', 75. Rabbi Emil Moses Cohn (who took as his pen name Emil Bernhard Cohn), was a staunch pro-Zionist whose political views led to his forced resignation from the Berlin synagogue in 1907. He did not return to Berlin until 1925.

57 Busch, *Unter dem Bogen*, 151.

58 K. Barth, 'Biblical Questions, Insights, and Vistas.' Lecture presented at the Aarau Student Conference, April 1920, in *WGWM*, 65.

59 L. Baeck, 'Die Existenz des Juden: Lehrausvortrag am 30.Mai 1935', in *Leo Baeck Institute Bulletin*, 81 (1988), 1. Cited in Busch, 'Indissoluble Unity', 73.

60 Friedman, 216, 218.

with Buber, Cohn and the Patmos Circle. More compelling than this—arguably circumstantial—evidence, is the evidence internal to Barth's dogmatic work that, far from modern Jewish thought being alien to him, he was at least aware of, and to a degree conversant with, its contemporary trends. In *CD* I/2, which Barth completed in the summer of 1937, he notes specifically the contributions to Old Testament scholarship of Martin Buber, Hans-Joachim Schoeps, and Emil Cohn, whose *Aufruf* he had already read.[61] These men are 'instructive to listen to', says Barth, 'both in what they say as earnest Jews, and in what they cannot say as unconverted Jews' [*CD* I/2, 80]. The slightly patronizing tone of this last comment should not be overstated. In the context of the section in which it occurs—§14.2, 'The Time of Expectation'—in which Barth outlines the revelational relationship between the Old and New Testaments, he is merely being consistent with his role as a Christian theologian. That there are things that even such eminent Jewish scholars as Buber and Schoeps cannot say with regard to christological connections between the Testaments is obvious—Barth acknowledges the boundary beyond which they cannot go, while also registering his appreciation for what their scholarship can say. There is, of course, the related question of precisely what Barth thought these writers were saying that was so instructive. Do they instruct him about his own theological tradition? Unlikely. Does he listen to them to be instructed about their theological traditions? Most doubtful. But are they instructive to him with regards to their understanding of God? Perhaps here is where Barth is, at this early stage of the Dogmatics, most ready to hear Jewish scholars.[62] Most interestingly, though, is that late in his life Barth became noticeably more appreciative of Buber, regarding him as biblically and theologically legitimate dialogue partner. Buber's I–Thou theology was, in Barth's mind, prefigured in the Old Testament prophets. Moreover, Buber 'was concerned…with the problem of the solidarity of God and my neighbour, my neighbour and God, and in this sense with the Kingdom of God…'[63] The similarity between this and key themes of Barth's thought are obvious.

If Barth was associated with certain Jews and contemporary Judaic theology in the pre-war years, there is also no doubt that he maintained his contact with Jewish organizations and individuals throughout the Nazi period, both before and after his expulsion from Germany. Gleaning this from the archival evidence is not, however, always a straightforward matter. In large part, it relies upon an appreciation of the nature of the relationship between Barth and his secretary, Charlotte von Kirchsbaum, who lived in the Barth household from 1929 until 1964. She was, in Barth's own words, his 'faithful helper…indispensable in every way', who took 'an

---

61 M. Buber, *Königtum Gottes*, 1932; H.-J. Schoeps, *Jüdischer Glaube in dieser Zeit*, 1932, and *Jüdisch-christliches Religiongespräch*, 1937; E.B. Cohn, *Judentum, ein Aufruf der Zeit*, 1934.

62 It is, I believe, significant that this section of *CD* I/2 in which he refers to Buber, Schoeps and Cohn concerns the unity of revelation in both Testaments that, regrettably for Barth, has been entirely ignored by the parlous state of recent Christian interpretation of the Old Testament. Indeed, his point is to argue that the most useful exegetical works on the Old Testament come from Jewish, not Christian, scholars.

63 K. Barth, 'Liberal Theology: Some Alternatives', *Hibbert Journal*, vol.59, no.3 (1961), 217–218. Cited in Pangritz, 145-146.

immeasurable part in [the] origin and progress' of the *Church Dogmatics* [*CD* IV/4, viii]. She was also a strong companion for Barth in his political resistance and, once in Switzerland, in his work on behalf of non-Aryan refugees. A few examples may help.

In 1935, the same year in which Barth was dismissed from his post in Bonn, the Basel government appointed him its Commissioner for Refugees. Barth undertook this role with passionate interest and involvement, providing financial support and opening his home to Jewish refugees from Germany. One such recipient of his aid was the celebrated pianist Rudolf Serkin, who fled to the USA via Barth's Swiss home, in 1939. In return for Barth's hospitality, Serkin gave free piano lessons to his daughter, Franziska![64] In fact, however, it was von Kirschbaum who, on Barth's behalf, shouldered much of the responsibilities of this position.

The situation was similar with the *Schweizerischen evangelischen Hilfswerkes für die bekennende Kirche in Deutschland*, founded in 1938. As part of her involvement with this organization, von Kirschbaum 'was in charge of [assisting] the oppressed members of the Confessing Church and…Christian-Jewish and Jewish refugees, working together with the Swiss Jewish refugee organization.'[65] In late 1938, for example, von Kirschbaum wrote to Pastor Paul Vogt on behalf of a Jewish-Christian girl in Berlin, Gerda Schmalz, for whom she was keen to acquire a visa for Switzerland. That her letter included greetings from Barth indicates not only that Barth was supportive of her work, but also that he was prepared to place himself at risk of incrimination in the event of this or other such letters being intercepted.[66] A similar letter was written by von Kirschbaum to Vogt in early 1939, on behalf of a Fräulein Stamm from Blumenthal—whom both von Kirschbaum and Barth knew—and a young Jew who had sought Stamm's help to cross the German–Swiss border.[67] Once again, the specific references to Barth and, indeed, to the Gestapo in relation to Stamm suggest that von Kirschbaum was writing to Vogt with Barth's knowledge and acquiescence. Through von Kirschbaum, Barth was also in close contact with the German lawyer Kurt Müller. According to Busch, Müller established a set of safe houses in Stuttgart for German Jews and was in constant but secret contact with the Barth household in connection with this work.[68]

Although Charlotte von Kirschbaum was coordinating these resistance activities, it is implausible to suggest that Barth was either unaware of or disinterested in

---

64 Busch, *Unter dem Bogen*, 269. See also F. Jehle, *Ever Against the Stream: The Politics of Karl Barth, 1906-1968*, trans. R. & M. Burnett, (Grand Rapids: Eerdmans, 2002), 57.

65 R. Palmer, 'Eberhard Busch on "Charlotte von Kirschbaum, the collaborator" ', in the *Karl Barth Society Newsletter*, (Spring, 2000), 7.

66 Letter, C. von Kirschbaum to Paul Vogt, 12 November 1938, Karl Barth-Archiv.

67 Letter, C. von Kirschbaum to Paul Vogt, 27 January 1939, Karl Barth-Archiv. It is instructive to note that Barth seems to have had no concerns about trusting his secretaries— both von Kirschbaum and, later, Busch—writing (not merely transcribing from dictation) letters and then simply handing them to Barth for his signature, as though they were in fact written by Barth himself. This adds weight to the suggestion that von Kirschbaum's letters on behalf of Jewish and Jewish-Christian refugees were indeed known to and fully supported by Barth. See Palmer, 6.

68 Busch, cited by Palmer, 8.

them—the very fact that she lived in Barth's house during the entire period of this conspiracy is enough to connect him with the aid-work by association. But mere vicarious involvement through his secretary is, in fact, not all that can be claimed for Barth. That he was as committed as von Kirschbaum to the rescue of Jews and Jewish-Christians can be demonstrated by the fact that it was under the auspices of the Swiss Evangelical Society for Aid that, on 5 December 1938, and in explicit response to *Kristallnacht*, Barth delivered his lecture 'Bekennende Kirche und politische Fragen von heute.' Invitations to the lecture were prefaced with the recognition of the recent 'dreadful consequences of the Jewish persecution in Germany', and it was in this lecture that Barth declared that 'antisemitism is a sin against the Holy Spirit.'[69] In Barth's view, the 'really decisive biblical-theological reason' for the Church's No! to National Socialism was Nazism's intrinsic antisemitism which 'precisely in these last few weeks has so especially moved us.'[70] If Barmen was silent on the 'Jewish question', Barth's 1938 Wipkingen address delivered a full and frank condemnation of Nazi antisemitism, not merely on behalf of Jewish-Christians but indeed for Jews per se.

Similarly, following his Wipkingen lecture, Barth was determined not to repeat the Confessing Church's failure to enact the political implications of Barmen. Thus, in April 1939, Barth met with Heinrich Grüber to discuss developments in Germany. In early June of the same year, Barth again had reason to have contact with Grüber, albeit under less pleasant circumstances. According to correspondence between von Kirschbaum and Pastor Rhenus Gelpke (Secretary of the Swiss Evangelical Aid Society's Sub-Commission for non-Aryan Christians), Grüber had sent a certain couple named Königshöfer from Berlin to Barth's house in Basel for safety, though without informing either Barth or von Kirschbaum beforehand. In spite of the fact that the situation—seemingly brought about by a lack of clear procedures—clearly caused Barth's entire household some perplexity, Barth was 'nonetheless prepared to write a letter of introduction' for the Königshöfers to assist them in getting safe passage.[71] Fully occupied with the work of his 'Buro Grüber', the Berlin pastor was later imprisoned in Sachsenhausen and Dachau for aiding and sheltering German Jews. After the war, he was the only German witness to appear for the prosecution at the 1961 trial of Adolf Eichmann.[72]

---

69 'Einladung', December 1938, Karl Barth-Archiv; K. Barth, 'Die Kirche und die politische Frage von heute', in K. Barth, *Eine Schweizer Stimme, 1938-1945*, (Zürich: Theologische Verlag, 1985), 90.

70 Barth, 'Die Kirche und die politische frage von heute', 89. See also M.R. Lindsay, *Covenanted Solidarity: The Theological Basis of Karl Barth's Opposition to Nazi Antisemitism and the Holocaust*, (New York: Peter Lang, 2001), 261–264.

71 Letter, C. von Kirschbaum to Pfr. Rhenus Gelpke, 7 June 1939, Karl Barth-Archiv.

72 Heinrich Grüber, later Dean of the Evangelical Church of East and West Berlin, has been criticized by Richard Rubenstein for espousing antisemitic theology. However, it is worth noting that Rubenstein also readily acknowledges Grüber's bravery, and that he was 'neither a Nazi nor an anti-Semite but a very decent human being…' The fundamental difficulty for Rubenstein was (and is) that Grüber's theological arguments were entirely logically consistent with 'the normative Judeo-Christian theology of covenant and election.' See Rubenstein, 3–4.

It is also quite possible that von Kirschbaum's friend Kurt Müller may have been the link between Barth and Helmut Hesse, the Lutheran pastor of Elberfeld. In mid-1943, Hesse proclaimed that:

> As Christians we can no longer tolerate the silence of the Church on the persecution of the Jews. What leads us to this conclusion in the simple commandment to love one's neighbour…The Jewish question is an evangelical, not a political, question. The Church has to resist antisemitism in its territories…and to stand up against the state to testify to…make every effort to oppose the destruction of Jewry.[73]

Only two days after making this statement, Hesse was arrested by the Gestapo and imprisoned in Dachau, where he died five months later. Busch contends that the statement that was read out by Hesse, and which subsequently led to his arrest, was delivered to Germany by Müller after having been formulated by Barth.[74]

There exists, in other words, overwhelming evidence to show that Barth was intimately involved with resistance efforts from Switzerland on behalf of Jews and Jewish-Christians. Moreover, it is clear that this involvement was based, not upon an abstract understanding of Israel, but indeed upon a very real engagement with individual Jews and Jewish organizations dating back at least to the days of his Safenwil pastorate. If further proof is needed, one need only consider the crucial role played by Barth in the heroic (but ultimately unsuccessful) efforts to halt the mass deportation of Hungarian Jews in 1944.

On 7 April 1944 Rudolf Vrba, a Slovakian Jew who had been a prisoner in Majdanek and then Auschwitz since June 1942, made a dramatic escape from Auschwitz-Birkenau, together with Alfred Wetzler, another Slovakian Jew. Unlike most previous escapees, Vrba and Wetzler managed to evade capture in the first critical hours and, by 21 April, had arrived safely in Slovak territory. Four days later they were in Zilina, compiling a detailed and graphic account of the conditions in Auschwitz, an estimate of the number of Jews already murdered and the means by which it was done, and a chilling warning of the impending deportation of Hungarian Jews. Once the report had been written, representatives of the Zilina and Bratislava Jewish Councils began the urgent—and highly secretive—task of disseminating it, first throughout Slovakia and Hungary, and then also to the Allied forces in the West. In the meantime, the Vrba–Wetzler report—or, the Auschwitz Protocol, as it came to be known—was corroborated by the accounts of two other Jews, Arnost Rosin and Czezlaw Mordowicz, who had escaped from Auschwitz on 27 May.

The various routes by which copies of the composite report were distributed were, perhaps necessarily, circuitous, and at least one copy ended up in the possession of the Budapest Gestapo. Another copy, however, made its way to Barth. Moshe Krausz, a member of the Palestine Office in Budapest, had sent a copy of the report to Florian Manoliu, a staffer in the Romanian Legation's Berne office. Manoliu then passed the report to Georges Mandel-Mantello—Acting First Secretary of the El Salvador Consulate in Geneva—who in turn distributed it to his own circle of

---

73 Hauptstaatsarchiv Düsseldorf, *Gestapoakten*, File No.47, 308. Cited in S. Gordon, *Hitler, Germans and the 'Jewish Question'*, (Princeton: Princeton University Press, 1984), 258.

74 Busch, cited by Palmer, 8.

influential people in Switzerland. One such individual was Rabbi Zwi Taubes from Zürich who, on 25 June, visited Barth and gave him a copy of Vrba's account.[75]

If Taubes had hoped that Barth would act on the information, he was not disappointed. On the same day that he received the report, Barth wrote to Bundesrat Nobs and the entire Federal Council asking urgently whether there was something that the Swiss authorities could do.

> For hundreds of thousands [in Hungary] all help is already too late, as it is for millions of fellow-Jews in Germany, France, Poland, Russia…Every day, a further thousand or ten thousand die in Hungary, and the same fate undoubtedly hangs over the whole [Jewish population]. In two, three weeks it will be all over. Yet it is not out of the question that a further hundred thousand could still be rescued.[76]

Having written this letter, Barth immediately began recruiting friends and allies to strengthen the cause. On 4 July, Barth wrote a second letter to the Federal Council, this time having it counter-signed by Paul Vogt, Emil Brunner and Willem Visser't Hooft.

> We are sending you two reports from Hungary and a covering letter, dated 19 June 1944, which originated from a wholly reliable source and has come to us via a diplomatic channel in Switzerland. The reports have shocked us most deeply. Out of our sense of duty, we are obliged to give you both reports…We do not doubt that you will take the trouble to read them and to circulate them among your circles.[77]

History records, of course, that while Swiss government policy altered from qualified neutrality to a more humane attitude toward Jewish refugees in the days and weeks following these two letters, the West's reaction was too late. By 9 July, when the Hungarian deportations stopped, all of Hungary—with the exception of Budapest—had been made *judenrein*. The intense campaign undertaken by the Swiss press and initiated, in part, by Barth's letters, had failed to stop 'the single most concentrated killing orgy at Auschwitz.'[78] Largely due to the dissemination of the Vrba-Wetzler report, in which Barth played a key role in Switzerland, there had been widespread and public foreknowledge among the Allied nations of the Nazis' plans for the Hungarian Jews. Yet nothing was done to prevent the catastrophe until it was all but over. In what was hopefully a retrospective acknowledgment of culpability, the Hungarian tragedy was later described by Winston Churchill as 'probably the greatest and most horrible crime ever committed in the history of the world.'[79]

---

75 According to Busch, Taubes had chosen to seek out Barth because he was a prominent Swiss advocate for the Jews. See Busch, *Unter dem Bogen*, 515n58.

76 Letter, K. Barth to Bundesrat E. Nobs, 25 June 1944, Karl Barth-Archiv. Cited in Busch, *Unter dem Bogen*, 515–516.

77 Letter, K. Barth *et al* to the Swiss Federal Council, 4 July 1944, Karl Barth-Archiv.

78 Goldhagen, 160.

79 R.L. Braham, 'The Holocaust in Hungary: A Retrospective Analysis', in Berenbaum & Peck, 434. For further details of the Vrba–Wetzler report, the Swiss press campaign and the destruction of the Hungarian Jews, see: Lindsay, *Covenanted Solidarity*, 267–269; R.L. Braham, *The Politics of Genocide: The Holocaust in Hungary*, 2 vols, (New York:

Conclusion

Evidently, there has been and remains a great deal of controversy, not to say confusion, surrounding Barth's personal attitudes toward Jews and Judaism. His own comments on this subject, made late in his life, have hardened the perception of his critics that he held deep-seated suspicion of and perhaps even animosity toward Jews. And yet, as we have seen, the historical record suggests a somewhat different story. Rather than espousing an ill-informed and abstract notion of 'the Jews', as has been argued by some, Barth in truth had significant relationships with individual Jews through whom he also became acquainted with contemporary Jewish thought. If, in the early 1920s, he kept these acquaintances at a respectable scholarly distance, the Nazi years—particularly as the persecution of the Jews intensified to genocidal proportions—saw him adopt a far more positive perspective, from which he was able to stand in both theological and humanitarian solidarity with the persecuted kinfolk of Jesus. In the words of Rabbi Geis, 'Who, other than Karl Barth, could have demonstrated more clearly the struggle and courageous resistance that develops from grace?'[80]

Columbia University Press, 1981); D.H. Kranzler, 'The Swiss Press Campaign that Halted Deportations to Auschwitz and the Role of the Vatican, the Swiss and Hungarian Churches,' in *Remembering for the Future*; D.H. Kranzler, *The Man Who Stopped the Trains to Auschwitz: Georges Mantello, El Salvador, and Switzerland's Finest Hour*, (Syracuse University Press, 2001).

80 R.R. Geis, '*Leiden an der Unerlöstheit der Welt: Briefe, Reden, Aufsätze*, ed. D. Goldschmidt & I. Überschär, (Munich, 1984), 240. Cited in Busch, 'Indissoluble Unity', 58.

Chapter Three

Karl Barth and Natural Theology: A case study of the Holocaust as a theological *locus*

To this point, this book has sought to adequately contextualize Barth by looking, in Chapter One, at the overall state of Jewish–Christian relations since 1945 and, in Chapter Two, at the extent of Barth's interaction with individual Jews. The argument thus far has been that Barth's role is far more complex and deeply nuanced than most commentators have to date allowed. If, for example, his dogmatic theology of Israel expresses a somewhat conflicted perspective—at times, wonderfully appreciative, yet elsewhere weighed down with caricatures and ill-considered stereotypes—this is no different to, and often better than, the course of Christian post-Holocaust theology generally. Similarly, despite his self-confessed visceral antipathy to Jews, and his regret that he did not do more to help them during the Nazi years, we have seen that in fact he was well-acquainted with both individual Jews and contemporary Jewish scholarship, and personally involved in efforts to rescue Jews from occupied countries.

In this chapter, though, we come at last to the start of our theological explorations. The evident ambiguity of Barth's personal relations with and feelings toward the Jewish people, at which we looked in the last chapter, is mirrored in the ambiguity of his response as a theologian to the events of the Holocaust. What his response was is, naturally, of great significance. As Arthur Cohen has put it, 'The *tremendum* cannot be avoided.'[1] In other words, how a given theology responds to, and integrates into itself, this most catastrophic of events within the life of the Jewish people is directly indicative of that theology's coherence. If, then, we can come to an understanding of how well Barth was able to respond theologically to the *Shoah*, we will have a clue as to how well the rest of his theology perceives Israel more broadly. In order to do this, though, we have first to ask how far Barth was prepared to allow history to have free interplay with theology.

It has been the widely, and at times carelessly, accepted wisdom that Barth's theological method denies any legitimate role to history in the task of theological construction. His complete repudiation of natural theology would seem to vindicate this assumption. As we shall see, however, Barth was not always so adamant in his rejection of natural theology. His very earliest theological work in fact betrays a somewhat different position. Consequently, and notwithstanding Barth's infamous

---

1   A. Cohen, *The Tremendum*, (New York: Crossroad, 1981), 36. The *tremendum* is how Cohen refers to the Nazi death camps.

Nein! to his erstwhile friend Emil Brunner, the way in which Barth reacted to the *Shoah*—without doubt the most decisive historical event in his life-time—suggests that in his later years he was prepared to adopt a more moderate view and allow for the possibility of some 'ordinary' history being, if not theologically decisive, at least theologically significant.

To make this claim is, in a sense, to go 'against the stream' of the general consensus amongst Barth scholars that Barth was the most resolute opponent of natural theology. As Stanley Hauerwas has put it in his own highly ironic Gifford Lectures, Barth's theology 'is a massive theological metaphysics that provides an alternative to the world in which Lord Gifford's understanding of natural theology seems reasonable.'[2] To claim, though, that Barth did eventually make limited room for the theological significance of some history is not of course to claim that he understood the Holocaust as *Geschichte*, as the 'real time' of God's revelation. While it has been cogently argued elsewhere that the Holocaust itself can and perhaps should be understood as an event of revelation, this is not at all what I would suggest Barth to have believed.[3] Indeed, I would go so far as to say that Barth did not seem capable or even willing to embed the lessons of the Holocaust deeply into his theology, at least insofar as they related to his doctrine of evil (*das Nichtige*). As John McDowell has recently written, *CD* III/3 (in which, of course, the exposition of *das Nichtige* is located) is an inevitable disappointment to any who would read it in the hope of finding 'Barth's commentary on, or even explicit theological response to, the cultural landscape' of the immediately post-Auschwitz world.[4] We would look to Barth in vain if we hoped to see in his post-war writings an example of the conviction that theology must never again be done 'in such a way that its construction remains unaffected…by Auschwitz.'[5]

To argue that Barth did come to accept that some 'ordinary' history can have theological significance is, nonetheless, to make the claim that the events of the Holocaust were of such a magnitude that not even he could in the end refuse to acknowledge their theological impact. Moreover, this acknowledgment had inevitable consequences for his theological, personal and political perception of the Jews and the State of Israel. The impact of these consequences on Barth's political relationship to the State of Israel will be explored in greater detail in Chapter Three. Chapter Five will consider the way in which his *Israellehre* as presented in *CD* IV was influenced. As groundwork, however, this chapter will explore Barth's opposition to natural theology in the context of the wider debate on the subject, and then question if (and the extent to which) Barth was forced to reconsider his position in the aftermath of the *Shoah*, in respect of his understanding of radical evil.

---

2   Hauerwas, 39.

3   See for example: M.R. Lindsay, 'History, Holocaust, and Revelation: Beyond the Barthian Limits', in *Theology Today*, 61 (January, 2005); E. Fackenheim, *God's Presence in History*, (New York, 1970); I. Maybaum, *The Face of God After Auschwitz*, (Amsterdam: Polak & Van Gennep, 1965).

4   J.C. McDowell, 'Much Ado About Nothing: Karl Barth's Being Unable to Do Nothing About Nothingness', in *IJST*, vol.4, no.3 (2002).

5   A.L. & A.R. Eckardt, cited in Z. Garber, *Shoah: The Paradigmatic Genocide*, Studies in the *Shoah*, vol.VIII, (Lanham: University Press of America, 1994), 1.

The Problem of Natural Theology

Christian theological history has, since its earliest days and especially over the past 150-odd years, been punctuated by a still-unresolved debate over whether or not history has a legitimate role in the construction of theological discourse. To what extent can and should history *as such* be used as determinative material for the theologian's task of reflecting upon and, where necessary re-configuring, Christian theology?

For the last few decades, names such as Reinhold Niebuhr, Wolfhart Pannenberg, Dietrich Ritschl, Delwin Brown and, to a lesser extent Stanley Hauerwas, have been central to the arguments surrounding the legitimacy of natural theology.[6] But the debate itself has been raging for centuries. As an ingredient to professional theological discourse, the controversy over natural theology's legitimacy was initially driven by an enhanced esteem granted to the discipline of history in the 1800s and the correlative scholarly popularity of the so-called quest for the historical Jesus. Begun by people like Hermann Samuel Reimarus in the late eighteenth century, the quest was epitomized in Schweitzer's seminal work from 1906. There was, indeed, a veritable plethora of various and varied 'lives of Jesus'. As John Kent has said, 'once Reimarus had shown that a coherent secular view of Jesus…was possible in terms of the New Testament evidence', a succession of 'radically different images of Jesus' emerged, ranging from those designed to affirm the orthodoxy, to those which were intended to liberate humanity either from Christianity itself (Renan, Nietzsche) or at least from its crippling dogmatism (Strauss, Schweitzer).[7] These and other developments led to the growth of the *Religionsgeschichtliche Schule* (History of Religions School) of biblical inquiry in the nineteenth century.[8] Leading disputants in the arena at that time included Albrecht Ritschl, Ernst Troeltsch and Julius Kaftan. Alongside them, stood the imposing figure of Friedrich Schleiermacher. According to him, 'history…is for religion the richest source…', and the contemplation of it by the pious mind shows it to be 'the greatest and most general revelation of the deepest and holiest.'[9]

Scholarship within Catholicism was also grappling with these issues at this time. Controversies stirred up by theological rationalists such as George Hermes (1775–1831) and Anton Günther (1783–1863), and by the fideism of Louis-Eugène-Marie Bautain (1796–1867) were chief among those with which the First Vatican Council in 1870 had to deal. It was in fact a deliberate strike against such movements

---

6   See for example: R. Niebuhr, *Faith and History: A Comparison of Christian and Modern Views of History*, (New York: Charles Scribner's Sons, 1949); W. Pannenberg (ed.), *Revelation as History*, (London: Macmillan, 1969); Ritschl, *The Logic of Theology*; D. Brown, *Boundaries of our Habitations*, (New York: SUNY Press, 1994); Hauerwas, *With the Grain of the Universe*.

7   J. Kent, in H. Cunliffe-Jones, (ed.), *A History of Christian Doctrine*, (Philadelphia: Fortress Press, 1980), 492.

8   See Albert Schweitzer's seminal work, *The Quest of the Historical Jesus: A Critical Study of its Progress from Reimarus to Wrede*, (Baltimore: The Johns Hopkins University Press, 1998).

9   F.D.E. Schleiermacher, cited in Mackintosh, 44ff.

that the First Vatican Council in 1870 dogmatized the old Thomist definition of natural theology, according to which 'God, the origin and end of all things, can be known with certainty by the natural light of reason from the things that he has made.'[10]

It was into this milieu that Barth was immersed as he began his theological studies. While his first four semesters in Berne were unutterably dry, in Berlin he found a haven with Harnack. It was also there that 'the possibility of understanding the Bible in terms of the history of religion began to dawn on me...'[11] Thus Barth came under the influence of Schleiermacher, whom he was 'inclined to believe... blindly all along the line.'[12]

When, in 1908, he moved to Marburg to complete his studies under Wilhelm Herrmann, he was introduced to an existentialized variant of Schleiermacher's theology. The religious rationalism of Hermann Cohen was an all-important factor in this. According to Cohen, the individual as a sinner cannot be redeemed from guilt by the moral commandment alone. Only the biblical concept of the correlation between humanity and God can solve this problem. For Cohen, then, revelation appears not as an historical event in the past, but as an eternal process of correlation between divine and human reason.[13]

It was precisely at this point that Herrmann could not agree with Cohen. Although committed to Marburg's neo-Kantian epistemology, Herrmann could not bring himself to accept Cohen's restricted vision of God as a merely ideal-logical correlation with humanity. In direct consequence of his debates with Cohen, and yet still working within the epistemological limits of neo-Kantianism, Herrmann was concerned to find a place for faith and divine revelation outside the Marburg *Religionsphilosophie*. God, he was convinced, was more than just a logical construct of the human mind. Similarly, God's own revelation was 'an actual, divine, and life-bestowing power...beyond consciousness.'[14] As with Cohen, this revelation was not 'historical' in the sense of being open to historical-critical method. But against Cohen, revelation was indeed related to the '*geschichtliche Tatsache*' of Jesus. However, the historicity of the revelation-event in Jesus was not an object of empirical study. Rather, the neo-Kantian Herrmann—and, therefore, the young Barth—supposed that the divine revelation was localized in Jesus' inner life.[15] Simon Fisher has summed up the Herrmannian adaptation of Cohen's epistemology as follows:

> When Herrmann talked about revelation being a *geschichtliche Tatsache* or of 'revelation entering our own temporal realm', he was speaking about [a] transcendental, moral, yet experiential life...History, accordingly, means something historic in the biographical life

---

10 '*Deum, rerum omnium principium et finum, naturali humanae rationis lumine e rebus creatis certo cognosci posse.*'

11 K. Barth, *Selbstdarstellung*, (1964), in Busch, *Karl Barth*, 40.

12 K. Barth, 'Nachwort', in H. Bolli (ed.), *Schleiermacher–Auswahl*, (Siebenstern Taschenbuch, 1968). Cited in Busch, *Karl Barth*, 40.

13 A. Shear-Yashuv, 'Jewish Philosophers on Reason and Revelation.' Paper presented at the Twentieth World Congress of Philosophy, (1998).

14 S. Fisher, 146.

15 McCormack, *Karl Barth's Critically Realistic Dialectical Theology*, 52–54, 61–63.

of the individual. History is not so much concerned with an event *wie es eigentlich gewesen war*, as with moral and religious facts (*Tatsachen*) and their significance for contemporary *Leben*...Revelation, as a historic fact, meant for Herrmann a religious experience which has importance for an individual's present and future moral comportment.[16]

The reliance on Cohen's privileging of ethics is clearly evident. But so too is the departure from Cohen's impersonal abstraction of God. So, as far as Barth was at this time concerned, faith was *Gotteserlebnis*, an 'immediate awareness of the presence and effectiveness of...the power of life.' Consequently, it was only by agreeing with Herrmann that Barth could affirm that faith is indeed the historical moment—but a moment that is mediated historically through the personality of Jesus as that personality is in turn actualized within human society.[17]

Between 1911 and 1914, however, Barth modified this emphasis on the inwardness of revelation to a model of revelation which enabled him to equate revelation with the actions of God on earth by which the Kingdom of God was realized. As McCormack puts it, while the 'theological foundation was still Herrmannian..., the superstructure had undergone drastic renovation.'[18] In his 1911 lecture, 'Jesus Christ and the Movement for Social Justice', for example, Barth argues that 'Jesus *is* the movement for social justice, and the movement for social justice *is* Jesus in the present.' This movement 'is not only the greatest and most urgent word of God to the present, but also in particular a quite direct continuation of the spiritual power which...entered into history and life with Jesus.'[19] Even in his sermons during the very early part of the First World War it is possible to detect something similar. So, for example, the theological significance of the war was that it represented God's judgmental No against Europe. But, as God's No, it was also—dialectically—His Yes, and thus the war was an instrument by which God's Kingdom was being realized.[20] This model of revelation, by now quite clearly distinct from Herrmann's inwardness, located Barth's thought within the domain of a 'dynamic eschatology', according to which he could posit a fluctuating relationship between revelation and some phenomenal-historical events.[21]

The crisis of the first war, however, forced Barth to reconsider his position entirely. Along with Eduard Thurneysen, Barth sensed the need to 'learn [his] theological ABC all over again...'[22] As he worked his way through *Romans* I and especially *Romans* II, he came to the conclusion that revelation does indeed become

---

16 S. Fisher, 150, 152.

17 K. Barth, 'Der Christliche Glaube und die Geschichte', in *Schweizerischer Theologische Zeitschrift*, 29 (1912), 5–7, 66.

18 McCormack, *Karl Barth's Critically Realistic Dialectical Theology*, 86.

19 K. Barth, 'Jesus Christ and the Movement for Social Justice', in G. Hunsinger (ed.), *Karl Barth and Radical Politics*, 19–20.

20 K. Barth, *Predigten, 1914*, U. & J. Fähler (eds), (Zürich: TVZ, 1974). See especially the sermons of 9 and 23 August 1914.

21 Note that this is not the use of the term 'dynamic eschatology' that von Balthasar employs. Rather, he uses the term to denote the irreversible movement in Christ of a doomed world order to a new order of life. See von Balthasar, 64.

22 Barth, 'Nachwort', 294*f.* Cited in Busch, *Karl Barth*, 97.

historical but only in the way that 'a tangent touches a circle' [*Rom* II, 30]. 'In so far as our world is touched in Jesus by the other world,' says Barth, 'it ceases to be capable of direct observation as history, time, or thing' [*Rom* II, 29]. With such a sharp distinction now being drawn by Barth between divine revelation and human–historical endeavour, it is no surprise that by the end of *Romans* II he has repudiated all attribution of theological significance to every conceivable ideology or principle. '[I]ndividualism, collectivism, nationalism, internationalism, humanitarianism, ecclesiasticism…Nordic enthusiasm [and] devotion to Western culture' are all so many 'high places' of idolatry and not at all to be identified with the movement of God in the world [*Rom* II].

When in 1921 Barth left Safenwil for his first teaching appointment in Göttingen and was required to prepare a course of dogmatics for the 1924–25 academic year, he found, through what McCormack calls 'a momentous discovery', the christological foundation for all that he had been trying to say in *Romans* II.[23] In Heinrich Heppe's *Reformed Dogmatics*, Barth chanced upon the ancient an-/enhypostatic christological formula. This proved to be a watershed discovery for him, as it compelled him to view revelation and history as, by their very natures, utterly distinct and yet also utterly united. 'The eschatological reservation which, in the phase of *Romans* II, had been safeguarded by the time–eternity dialectic, *was now built into the very structure of his Christology.*'[24] It was now possible for Barth to affirm that in Christ it is *truly* God who meets us, and also God who truly meets *us* [*GD*, 138–139].[25]

The Göttingen cycle of dogmatics, representing the only one of the three series of dogmatics that Barth ever finished (the other two being the 'false start' in Münster[26] and the Bonn–Basel *Church Dogmatics*) is more than simply a summary of Barth's early theology. Notwithstanding the changes that he made in his thinking between Göttingen and Bonn, the *Göttingen Dogmatics* make clear that there exists 'a deep, coherent logic that informs Barth's theology, early and late…'[27] By the 1930s, then, having formally adopted the Chalcedonian formula into his Christology, Barth's theology of revelation had developed to the point where he could state that, 'from the side of revelation itself absolutely everything speaks against the possibility of revelation becoming an event…' [*CD* I/2, 48]. Of course, revelation miraculously does indeed become an event. However, it does so as 'God's own time [and thus as] real time', in direct contrast to human time [*CD* I/2, 49]. So, to even debate the extent to which history may be commensurate with God's time of revelation rested, for the post-*Romans* Barth, 'upon a portentous failure to appreciate the nature of revelation' [*CD* I/2, 56]. The Barthian premise was by this stage insistent that the miraculous 'becoming an event' of revelation may indeed 'signify that revelation becomes

---

23 McCormack, *Karl Barth's Critically Realistic Dialectical Theology*, 327.

24 McCormack, *Karl Barth's Critically Realistic Dialectical Theology*, 328. Emphasis in original.

25 For a more detailed discussion of the evolution of Barth's understanding of revelation after 1919, see Lindsay, *Covenanted Solidarity*, 143–155.

26 Barth, *Die christliche Dogmatik im Entwurf: Die Lehre vom Worte Gottes. Prolegomena zur christlichen Dogmatik*, (Munich: Christian Kaiser Verlag, 1927; rev.edn Zürich: TVZ, 1982).

27 D.L. Migliore, 'Karl Barth's First Lectures in Dogmatics: *Instruction in the Christian Religion*', *GD*, LXI.

history' but never signifies that history becomes revelation [*CD* I/2, 58]. To word it otherwise, 'history is a predicate of revelation, [but] revelation is not a predicate of history' [*CD* II/2, 58].[28] At least in this respect, Barth was thoroughly un-dialectical; here, there is no ceaseless to-ing and fro-ing between two fundamentally equal poles (of history and revelation), such as may characterize the so-called 'complementary dialectic'.[29] Rather, even when qualified by the admission of miraculous space–time epiphanies of revelation, there was a radical privileging by Barth of the revelation of God over against the historical time of humanity.

It was in this context that the infamous correspondence between Karl Barth and Emil Brunner occurred in 1934, over Brunner's search for an *Anknüpfungspunk* ('point of contact') between God and humanity, revelation and reason. At a time when Nazism was claiming revelatory significance for itself, Brunner dangerously suggested that 'the task of our theological generation is to find a way back to a legitimate natural theology.' As John Hart has demonstrated, this was not the first disagreement between Barth and Brunner but rather the awful climax to a personal and theological estrangement that had been evident since the mid-1910s.[30] No matter how closely linked revelation and history had been in Barth's earliest theological explorations, by 1934 he was committed to a radically different position. Having authored in May the Barmen Declaration and, in that document, utterly rejecting the legitimacy of natural theology, Barth could do nothing other than issue a vehement *Nein!*, shattering forever his friendship with Brunner, and highlighting the divisiveness of this issue as never before.[31]

Of course, it was precisely Barth's distinction between revelation and history that enabled him to author the Barmen Declaration of 1934 and thus to issue such a strong voice of protest against the prevailing *völkisch* theology of Nazism and the *Deutsche Christen* that self-consciously attempted to integrate the revelation of God with the advent of Hitler. On the other hand, Barth himself reminds us that theology is a distinctly human endeavour, one of the 'humanistic sciences' which, precisely because its subject is God, must therefore be a '*modest* theology.'[32] As a consequence, theology must be contextualized, and so appropriate theological expression in one era may be inappropriate in another. In the post-Holocaust world, theological thought itself, and not simply individual doctrines, is susceptible to the challenge of re-contextualization. The magnitude of the Holocaust as an event that has shattered previous theological thinking is such that Barth's theology, perhaps precisely because it has been so influential, cannot be distanced from it.

The essential premise of this chapter, therefore, is that Barth's disavowal of natural theology, so vital during the German *Kirchenkampf*, was (and is) less

---

28 See also *GD*, 59–61.

29 M. Beintker, *Die Dialektik in der 'dialektischen Theologie' Karl Barths*, (Munich: Christian Kaiser Verlag, 1987).

30 J.W. Hart, 'The Barth–Brunner Correspondence', in Hunsinger, *For the Sake of the World*, 19–43.

31 See E. Brunner, *Natur und Gnade* (1934), and K. Barth, 'Nein! Antwort am Emil Brunner', in *Theologische Existenz heute*, 9, (Tübingen: Mohr, 1934).

32 K. Barth, *Evangelical Theology: An Introduction*, (London: Collins, 1965), 9,11.

helpful in the war's aftermath. If, as Denys Turner has recently stated, 'there can scarcely be [in our times] a theological proposition *less* likely to meet with approval' than that from Vatican I decreeing the importance of nature and reason,[33] then it must be countered that, insofar as the natural world includes the historical, this is exactly the sort of proposition that, in a post-*Shoah* world, needs to be revived. The corresponding question posed by this premise thus becomes whether or not Barth's rejection of natural theology disempowered him from adjusting his theology and therefore politics in the wake of the Holocaust.

Within contemporary Jewish theology, it is perhaps not surprising that many of the most influential thinkers have radically incorporated the Holocaust into theological discourse as a fundamentally determinative historical event. Emil Fackenheim, for example, articulates the Holocaust as an 'epoch-making event'; an event that, like the destruction of the First and Second Temples, challenges Jewry's collective conscious and compels it to respond to unprecedented situations in a way that nonetheless affirms the presence and providence of God. As Steven Katz paraphrases, 'Auschwitz itself is revelatory, commanding, and we must learn to sense what God would reveal to us even there.'[34]

In recent (Western) Christianity, Fackenheim's contention that the Holocaust is a fundamental theological issue—for Christians as well as Jews—is now hardly contentious at all. Thanks to the work of theologians such as John Roth, John Pawlikowski, Franklin Littell, Dietrich Ritschl and Jürgen Moltmann, not only the legitimacy but indeed the necessity of Holocaust studies within doctrinal reflection has been assured. The memory of the Six Million has thus made revelation deeply—and traumatically—historical.

But this was not the case in 1945—and so what about Barth, who was in the twilight of his theological career by the time serious theological reflection upon the Holocaust became commonplace? Is it possible that his post-Safenwil refusal to allow historical events to be constructive elements in theological discourse was modified, at least in part, by the *Shoah*? If there was a moderation of his repudiation of natural theology, what role, if any, did any reflections of his on the *Shoah* play in affecting the change? Before attempting an answer to that question in respect of Barth's attitude toward the Jews and the State of Israel, it may be useful to consider whether or not the *Shoah* influenced his understanding of another key doctrine that, for many, has required substantial revision since 1945—the problem of evil.[35]

---

33 D. Turner, *Faith, Reason and the Existence of God*, (Cambridge: Cambridge University Press, 2004), 3. My emphasis.

34 S. Katz, *Post-Holocaust Dialogues: Critical Studies in Modern Jewish Thought*, (New York: New York University Press, 1983), 208. Eliezer Berkovits is one of the few Jewish theologians, and arguably the most prominent, for whom the *Shoah* does not raise original issues.

35 As an aside, it should be said that the intention of this chapter is directed specifically at the ways in which Barth allowed—or did not allow—his historical context to inform his understanding of the problem of evil itself. It is not the intention to explore the myriad ways in which evil and the Holocaust have impacted upon Christian and Jewish theology in general throughout the past three decades, particularly through the works of scholars such as Richard Rubenstein, Katharina von Kellenbach and Henry Knight. Renegotiation of traditional doctrines such as covenant, election and revelation are key to this broader topic but cannot,

The Holocaust and the Doctrine of Evil

It is surely incontestable that the problem of evil is one of the most perplexing issues with which humankind is and always has been confronted, irrespective of religious faith or unbelief. Within the Christian tradition, in which the idea of a fundamentally benevolent God is central, the dilemma has been perhaps even more problematic. Augustinian theodicy, whereby evil is ascribed to humanity's misuse of its freedom to choose between good and evil, has been the Church's most familiar (and defensive) response. Irenaean, Process and 'protest' theodicies are, though, ample proofs that Christian theology is far from holding a consensual view. The debate itself is not new. As the names of the some of the theological responses listed above show, Church Fathers as far back as Augustine (354–430 CE) and Irenaeus (*c*130–*c*200 CE) were struggling to come to a solution that was both internally coherent and biblically sustainable. Before them, Socrates was defining evil (somewhat unsatisfactorily) as ignorance.[36] Through the Holocaust, however, the ultimate insufficiency of all Christian responses has been illuminated as never before. The difficulties of comparative genocide studies notwithstanding, nowhere in recent history has the profundity of radical evil been disclosed in all its inhumanity than in the machinations of the Nazi death camps. They were, as Otto Friedrich has put it, 'world[s] unlike any other because [they] were created and governed according to the principles of absolute evil.'[37]

There have, of course, been events in more recent history, as well as events much further back, which have taught a similar lesson. One could suggest, for example, Torquemada's indiscriminate Inquisition in the fifteenth and sixteenth centuries, the brutal suppression of the indigenous peoples in both Australia and the Americas by European colonists, the ideological terror of Stalin's rule, and the savagery of the Rwandan and Cambodian killing fields. It would be historical arbitrariness of the worst sort if these events were ignored, and most serious scholars of genocide studies now routinely include these horrors in the same broad spectrum that also includes the Holocaust. Equally, the willful intentionality of the 9/11 terrorists brought the reality of profound evil into the lives and, through television sets the living rooms, of 'ordinary people' throughout the world. Nonetheless, it was the *Shoah* that put the particular lesson of radical evil and its various manifestations squarely on the curriculum. As Dietrich Ritschl has said, Auschwitz stands as the 'paradigm of evil and suffering in our time.'[38] Indeed, the very fact that the language of genocide has taken its place within historical, legal, philosophical and theological discourse is largely due to the Holocaust.[39]

---

by virtue of their scope, be adequately covered here. For an excellent summary of where current discussion stands, see Roth & Maxwell, *Remembering for the Future*. Especially also, Rubenstein, *After Auschwitz*.

36 See for example, S. Kierkegaard, *The Sickness Unto Death*, trans. W. Lowrie, (Princeton: Princeton University Press, 1973), 218*ff*.

37 O. Friedrich, *The Kingdom of Auschwitz*, (London: Penguin, 1996), 100.

38 Ritschl, 38.

39 Interview with Jonathan Steinberg, *Limina*, vol.3, (1997), 3–4.

Thus if theologians and ecclesiastics have traditionally taught the all-pervasiveness of sin on the human condition, it has been the Holocaust of the Jews which has given to that doctrine its most violent validation to date, and which has reinforced an understanding of the extent to which all of humanity is its potential victim and/or agent. As Christopher Browning and Daniel Jonah Goldhagen have shown, the systematic extermination of over six million humans, solely on account of their race, was perpetrated by 'ordinary men'.[40] Of the sadistic doctors like Josef Mengele, for example, Robert Jay Lifton notes that they were 'neither brilliant nor stupid, neither inherently evil nor particularly ethically sensitive, they were by no means the demonic figures...people have often thought them to be.'[41] There can be no hiding behind the myth that this was a crime committed by inhuman monsters. Rather, as Stanley Milgram's experiments from 1961–62 showed, all people stand vulnerable to, and culpable for, evil. It is in the context of this extreme universality of evil which, during the Holocaust, transformed 'ordinary men' into murderers, that one can understand why Hannah Arendt perceived this evil to be so commonplace that, the magnitude of its results notwithstanding, it was in itself paradoxically banal.

The *Shoah* has, in other words, simultaneously justified our perennial concern with the question of evil, and by its enormity placed a question-mark against all previous answers. But to what extent did Karl Barth's own answer, formulated in terms of *das Nichtige* (Nothingness) and only a few short years after the Holocaust, appropriate the lessons of that cataclysm and enable him to take with greater seriousness the role of history in theological construction, and with greater sensitivity the ongoing role of the Jews in the covenant of God?

Barth is not, of course, the only one since 1945 to have explored the idea of radical evil. Nor is this the first time that Barth's concept of *das Nichtige* has been subjected to critical scrutiny. John McDowell's article has already been mentioned. Nicholas Wolterstorff, too, has published a review of Barth's doctrine from the point of view of philosophical theology.[42] Where Wolterstorff's article falls short, however, is in its complete lack of historical contextualization, without which the concept of Nothingness is robbed of its potency. Similarly, R. Scott Rodin has also published on this topic, although for him, the *locus* of evil in the architecture of Barth's theology is to be found in Barth's doctrine of God, rather than in his concept of *das Nichtige*.[43] While this approach may uncover a richer picture of Barth's doctrine overall, it does not and cannot take into account the impact of the Holocaust on that doctrine, as

---

40 C.R. Browning, *Ordinary Men: Reserve Police Battalion 101 and the 'Final Solution' in Poland*, (New York: Aaron Asher Books, 1992); Goldhagen, *Hitler's Willing Executioners*. It is worth noting that the controversy with which Goldhagen's book has been surrounded has not primarily been because of his contention that much of the German populace was implicated in the Holocaust. Rather, it has been his suggestion that a psycho-social 'eliminationist antisemitism' was the *sole cause* of the genocide that has provoked the backlash.

41 R.J. Lifton, *The Nazi Doctors: Medical Killing and the Psychology of Genocide*, (New York, 1986). Cited in Berenbaum & Peck, 239.

42 N. Wolterstorff, 'Barth on Evil', *Faith and Philosophy*, vol.13, no.4 (1996), 584–608.

43 R. Scott Rodin, *Evil and Theodicy in the Theology of Karl Barth*, (New York: Peter Lang, 1997). Barth's Doctrine of God, found in *CD* II, was written between the summer of 1939 and the winter of 1941–42, and published in March 1942.

the doctrine of God—*Church Dogmatics* II—was completed before the end of the Second World War, and indeed even before the Holocaust itself got fully under way. Again, it is the interface of the theology and the history that is lacking, and which this chapter seeks to pick up.

So when faced with the unspeakable horror of the Holocaust, what did Barth in fact find it possible to say? It is pertinent at the outset to remember that, far from advocating a transcendentalized theology, centred upon a 'wholly other' God, that had only scant relevance to socio-political realities, Barth was a vocal opponent of the Hitler regime from the earliest days of Nazism. In 1935, Barth was deported from Germany to Switzerland for refusing to bow to what he regarded as the idolatrous demands of the Third Reich. For the next ten years, Barth championed the cause of the anti-Nazi resistance and, on the basis of his theology, actively involved himself in the efforts to rescue Jews. The nexus between theological presuppositions and political praxis which characterized his entire career was, in other words, perhaps most clearly articulated during the Nazi era.[44] This being the case, it would hardly be surprising if we were to find that the explication of evil, which Barth formulated between 1948 and 1950 as part of his 'Doctrine of Creation' (*CD* III/3), took into account the ghastly realities of Nazism and the Holocaust which were, at that time, still uppermost in Europe's collective memory. But is this in fact what we see?

There is no doubt that Barth's doctrine of *das Nichtige*, as the non-willed reality on the margins of God's creation and providence, represents one of the most remarkable attempts in theological history to comprehend the problem of evil. According to Barth's Roman Catholic commentator, Hans Urs Von Balthasar, by framing this problem of evil in strictly theological terms, he has taken it 'more seriously than [any] purely human experience or philosophical reflection [has ever done].' [45] The chronological proximity to the Holocaust perhaps helps to explain why. With the most traumatic event in recent history—which, in a very real sense, embodied evil as never before—still only a few short years in the past, the development of a concept of radical evil that could meet this challenge was desperately needed as an at least partial attempt to understand what had happened, and why. Thus, if Polman rejects Barth's doctrine as heretical on the grounds that it is unbiblical speculation,[46] it can be countered that the very magnitude of the Holocaust as an event that critiques the entire theological heritage of Christianity, required (and requires!) nothing less than speculative reasoning freed from the bonds of rigid orthodoxy.

To this extent, if Barth's doctrine is a product of *eisegesis* rather than *exegesis*, this could arguably be exactly the approach needed to formulate an understanding of evil that takes the Holocaust into serious account. When we come to Barth's explication itself, however, we are confronted with more than just speculation. As Mallow

---

44 See for example: Lindsay, *Covenanted Solidarity*; Busch, *Unter dem Bogen*.

45 Von Balthasar, 231.

46 A.D.R. Polman, *Barth*, trans. C. Freeman, (Grand Rapids: Baker Book House, 1960), 66–67, in V.R. Mallow, *The Demonic: An Examination into the Theology of Edwin Lewis, Karl Barth, and Paul Tillich*, (Lanham: University Press of America, 1983), 96. See also J. Hick, *Evil and the God of Love*, (New York: Harper & Row, 1966), 141–142. See also *CD* IV/3.1, 178.

says, the concept of Nothingness contains elements 'which are so far removed from traditional theological thought patterns that they raise the question as to whether it is possible to enter…into [Barth's] thinking…' at all.[47] In part, of course, this is not so much a function of any confused ontology, but of the concept of Nothingness itself. According to Barth, *all* theology is piecemeal and fractured, in that it is an attempt to state the perfection of God through the fundamentally imperfect medium of human language.[48] In trying to present the idea of evil however, the difficulty becomes more acute, because it is at this place above all that one encounters the abyss between God and humanity. Here especially, therefore, theology must speak 'in broken thoughts and utterances' [*CD* III/3, 294]. Nevertheless, if we are to reach an answer to our question, we must now attempt to comprehend these broken thoughts and, in so doing, enter into Barth's thought-world.

Outline of a Doctrine

Barth begins by contending that, alongside the existence of God and His creation, there exists a 'third factor' that can only be comprehended as an alien element at the margins of creation and providence. The malignant character of this alien factor is attested, immediately and without reservation, when Barth depicts it as 'an entire sinister system' that exists only in the form of 'opposition and resistance'. Although *das Nichtige* is 'unable to overwhelm and destroy [humankind]'—for reasons we shall shortly come to—'it constantly threatens and corrupts it' [*CD* III/3, 289–290]. As John Hick has noted, Barth perceives evil in its full seriousness as 'the object of unqualified fear and loathing' which 'takes the forms of sin and pain, suffering and death'[49] [*CD* III/3, 349].

We have not yet, however, arrived at a definition of what this alien element is. Properly speaking, we cannot talk of Nothingness as something which 'is'. In strictly ontological terms, '[o]nly God and His creature really and properly are' [*CD* III/3, 349]. This cannot be taken to imply that Nothingness does not exist. Indeed, Barth is singularly outspoken in his insistence that Nothingness has a terrifyingly real existence. Alan Davies is correct, therefore, to state that neo-orthodox theology, of which Barth was a founding member, 'was named after the old orthodoxy… partly because it resurrected the hoary orthodox doctrine of original sin…'[50] So, irrespective of whatever faults Barth's doctrine may contain, 'its author cannot be accused of taking too mild a view…'[51]

Nevertheless, Nothingness cannot be regarded as having an existence that merely parallels that of creation in an antithetical sense. Such an assumption would imply

---

47 Mallow, 45.

48 Karl Barth, 'The Word of God and the Task of the Ministry', in *WGWM*, 186; *CD* I/1.

49 Hick, *Evil and the God of Love*, 136, 138.

50 A. Davies, 'Evil and Existence: Karl Barth, Paul Tillich and Reinhold Niebuhr Revisited in the Light of the *Shoah*', in S.L. Jacobs (ed.), *Contemporary Christian Religious Responses to the Shoah*, Studies in the *Shoah*, vol.VI, (Lanham: University Press of America, 1993), 16.

51 Davies, 18.

that Nothingness is simply that which is not. Barth, however, rejects this suggestion, because the 'nots' of creation are essential to creation's perfection. 'God is God and not the creature, but this does not mean that there is nothingness in God. On the contrary, this "not" belongs to His perfection' [*CD* III/3, 349].[52] Similarly for the creature, the fact that it is the creature and not God is intrinsic to its creaturely perfection. Within the realm of creation, there exists light and dark, land and water. There is, in other words, a negative side as well as a positive side. There is

> not only a Yes but also a No; not only a height but also an abyss; not only clarity but also obscurity…; not only growth but also decay; not only opulence but also indigence; not merely beauty but also ashes; not only beginning but also end… [*CD* III/3, 295, 296–297]

This shadow-side is, however, as much a part of the perfection of creation as the positive side. To equate it with Nothingness is no less than blasphemy [*CD* III/3, 349].[53]

In what sense, therefore, can we speak of Nothingness as an existing reality? According to Barth, the ontic context of its existence is the divine activity of creation grounded in election. In *CD* III/1, §41, Barth posits the view that the work of creation is presupposed by God's decision of election. Thus, he regards 'creation as the external basis of the covenant', and the 'covenant as the internal basis of creation.' Later on in this volume, he explains that 'God the Creator did not say No, nor Yes and No, but Yes to what He created…Creation as such is not rejection, but election and acceptance' [*CD* III/1, 330–331]. It is this understanding that informs Barth's concept of the existential content and being of Nothingness. This does not mean that it is possible to explain the origin of evil in the world, as though it had an independently legitimate existence.[54] Rather, it is that which God did not elect to create but, rather, passed over. It is that 'from which God separates Himself and in the face of which He…exerts His positive will' [*CD* III/3, 351]. Put in another way, it is the object of *permittere*—God's permission—rather than of *efficere*, which is God's direct production. In electing and, therefore, in subsequently creating what He elected, Nothingness was passed over by God, as that which He did not will and thus did not create: 'God elects, and therefore rejects what he does not elect. God wills, and therefore opposes what he does not will. He says Yes, and therefore says No to that to which He has not said Yes' [*CD* III/3, 351]. It is on the basis of this non-willing that Nothingness exists. It exists, that is to say, as 'what God did not, and does not and cannot will. It has the essence only of non-essence and only as such can it exist' [*CD* III/3, 352]. Precisely in this way, however, it does exist.

In this regard, we are faced squarely with the paradoxical situation whereby, as Mallow has correctly read Barth to say, the only context in which Nothingness

---

52 See also Von Balthasar, 228.

53 Barth thus directly refutes Leibniz who regards metaphysical evil as 'simply the non-divinity of the creature…' Thus, it is not a positive evil, but merely a 'deficiency or "privation" proper to the creature' (p.316).

54 G.C. Berkouwer, *The Triumph of Grace in the Theology of Karl Barth*, trans. H.R. Boer, (Grand Rapids: Eerdmans, 1956), 216.

can exist is that of 'ontological impossibility' [*CD* IV/3.1, 178*f*].[55] God has neither willed nor created it, nor does it have any source of existence independent of God (for as Barth insists, God 'is the basis and Lord of nothingness too' [*CD* III/3, 351]). Nevertheless, it exists. Certainly, it exists in its own *sui generis* form of malignancy and perversion, and as that of which 'God is wholly and utterly not the Creator...' [*CD* III/3, 352]. As an objective reality that threatens the creature, however, its existence cannot be gainsaid.

In moving from generalities to specifics, Barth regards the great evil of Nothingness as being, in its most exact formulation, the enemy of divine grace. Once again, this is most readily perceived if we recall the *loci* of election and creation as the presuppositions for any discussion of *das Nichtige*. Because God's activity as Creator is founded on His decision to elect, this decisive activity, as His *opus proprium*, is the work of divine grace. But Nothingness exists as that which is non-willed and, therefore, rejected. Evil 'is', in other words, only in its determination as that which is opposed to grace. As the reality which 'God does not will [but] negates and rejects', it exists only as 'the object of His *opus alienum*.' As such, it is the 'being that refuses and resists and therefore lacks His grace' [*CD* III/3, 353].

Two corollaries follow. First, as that which resists and hence lacks grace, Nothingness is the truest embodiment of evil (with the caveat that, once again, we are confronted with an oxymoron; Nothingness is 'true evil' only in the sense that it is the most authentic representation of falsehood [*CD* III/3, 525]). In spite of the ontic possibility in which Nothingness exists, we cannot argue that evil as such is rendered harmless. On the contrary, in its form of evil and death, Nothingness encounters humanity as 'affliction and misery', in face of which 'the creature is already defeated and lost.' According to Barth, there can be no avoiding the fact that the evil of Nothingness is constantly poised at the frontier of creation, threatening it and making it its victim. We must not be guilty, Barth says, of 'an easy, comfortable and dogmatic underestimation of its power in relation to us' [*CD* III/3, 293–295, 352, 254, 258]. 'The conquest of evil does *not* have that "matter-of-courseness" for man [*sic*] which it has for God.'[56] It therefore becomes clear why Barth so rigorously critiques Leibniz and Schleiermacher who, in Barth's opinion, are guilty of precisely this underestimation. Leibniz's definition of metaphysical evil as merely the imperfection of the creature represents, for Barth, a domestication of the adversary; because this imperfection is natural to the creature and thus belongs to its creaturely perfection, evil comes to be regarded simply as 'a particular form of good...' [*CD* III/3, 318]. Similarly with Schleiermacher, who in this context follows Irenaus, evil is 'correlative to good'. It exists in radical but not autonomous opposition to grace, in such a way that it is given 'a legitimate standing' as the 'counterpart and concomitant of grace.' Nothingness is, therefore, to be understood positively, and as that without which grace could not exist. To the extent that Schleiermacher understands it this way, as an indispensable counterpart to grace, it is not evil with which he is concerned

---

55 Mallow, 46. Evil therefore has an 'existence' which is 'enigmatic, inexplicable, absurd.' Berkouwer, 216.

56 Berkouwer, 221.

[*CD* III/3, 332–333]. In the face of these two views, the genuinely and dangerously evil character of Barth's *das Nichtige* stands out in sharp relief.

The second corollary is that, as the enemy of divine grace, Nothingness is primarily an assault upon God, with humanity as only the secondary target. Again, this is in contrast to Schleiermacher's doctrine, according to which the sovereignty of God elevates him above all violations.[57] For Barth, however, the conflict with Nothingness is primarily and properly God's own affair. Nothingness is the assault of the non-willed reality against the elected creation. As such, it represents an attack not only upon God's created covenantal partner but also and primarily upon God's decision to elect and, therefore, on God Himself. In *CD* II/2, Barth makes clear that, in pre-temporal eternity, God is an electing God. '[I]n the act of love which determines His whole being God elects.' Moreover, the act of election 'is not one moment with others in the prophetic and apostolic testimony', but, enclosed 'within the testimony of God to Himself, it is the moment which is the substance and basis of all other moments in that testimony' [*CD* II/2, 76, 91]. This being the case, the violation by Nothingness of the act and decision of election is as such a violation of God. This means that God, in faithfulness to the covenant, must take up the battle against Nothingness. He must be 'the Adversary of the adversary' [*CD* III/3, 357], otherwise He would not be true, either to His covenant partner or to Himself. As Barth puts it,

> We have not to forget the covenant, mercy and faithfulness of God, nor should we overlook the fact that God did not will to be God for His own sake alone, but that as the Creator He also became the covenant Partner of His creature, entering into a relationship with it in which He wills to be directly and [primarily] involved in all that concerns it…[This] means that whatever concerns and affects the creature concerns and affects Himself, not indirectly but directly, not subsequently and incidentally but primarily and supremely. Why is this so? Because, having created the creature, He has pledged His faithfulness to it. The threat of nothingness to the creature's salvation is primarily and supremely an assault upon His own majesty. [*CD* III/3, 356]

Barth is not thereby implying that God Himself is essentially threatened and corrupted by Nothingness, as humanity is. The counterpart of humanity's vulnerability to the power of *das Nichtige*, which we have already seen, is that we must not *over*estimate its power in relation to God. Indeed, if its power should be rated 'as high as possible in relation to ourselves', it must be rated 'as low as possible in relation to God' [*CD* III/3, 293, 295]. Nevertheless, God is not unmoved by radical evil. On behalf of His creation—which, in its encounter with Nothingness can only show itself to be the impotent victim of suffering—God opposes, confronts and victoriously crushes His graceless adversary. As may be expected from such a consistently christocentric theologian, the locus of this triumph over evil is the incarnation or, more specifically, the cross and resurrection of Christ.

At this place, we must qualify our earlier comment that God is not threatened by Nothingness. In the incarnation, God Himself becomes a creature and thus takes

---

57 'As Schleiermacher sees it, God has no part in this matter…He merely sees to it that we become conscious of [evil]' *CD* III/3, 329.

upon Himself the creature's sin, guilt and misery. In 'what befalls this man God pronounces His No to the bitter end.' The entire fury of Nothingness—and of God's wrath directed towards it—falls upon Christ 'in all its dreadful fulness…' [*CD* III/3, 362]. Precisely, however, because this *man* is also *God*, 'Nothingness could not master this victim.' It

> had power over the creature. It could contradict and oppose it and break down its defenses. It could make it its slave and instrument and therefore its victim. But it was impotent against the God who humbled Himself, and Himself became a creature, and thus exposed Himself to its power and resisted it [*CD* III/3, 362].[58]

By confronting and decisively triumphing over Nothingness in Jesus Christ, God has relegated it to the past. In the light of the cross and the empty tomb, 'there is no sense in which it can be affirmed that nothingness has any objective existence…' [*CD* III/3, 363]. Barth rejects outright the suggestion that radical evil exists in the form of an eternal antithesis. On the contrary, he insists that it has no perpetuity. It is neither created by God, nor maintained in a covenantal relationship with Him. Thus, 'we should not get involved in the logical dialectic that if God loves, elects and affirms eternally he must also hate and therefore reject and negate eternally. There is nothing to make God's activity on the left hand as necessary and perpetual as His activity on the right' [*CD* III/3, 360–361]. Nothingness has been brought to its end, no longer having even the transient and temporary existence it once had. On this note of 'cosmic optimism',[59] Barth concludes his presentation of his doctrine.

An Evaluation

Now that Barth's concept of radical evil has been sketched in brief outline, how must it be evaluated? In particular, how does it stand up to the challenge thrown out against all orthodoxies by the Holocaust? As a piece of theology that revolutionizes previous formulations of evil, it is perhaps not surprising that it has drawn significant criticism. Chief among the problems which scholars have raised is that of Barth's apparently confused ontology. Mallow finds it difficult to understand how Nothingness which, as that which God negates and therefore has no proper being, can nevertheless 'exist'.[60] Hick raises a similar point when he queries why God, in the positive act of creation had, *in logical necessity*, also to create the 'third factor' of Nothingness. Why can we not conceive of a God who is able to create a good universe 'that is not accompanied by the threatening shadow of rejected evil?' Why must God choose good and reject evil, as though these realities were existences 'which already [stood] in some way before Him…?'[61] The whole perplexing statement of the issue is simply 'a product of Barth's own fertile and imaginative mind.'[62]

---

58 See also *CD* II/2, §35.

59 Davies, 20.

60 Mallow, 97.

61 Hick, *Evil and the God of Love*, 142–143, 192–193.

62 Hick, *Evil and the God of Love*, 149.

For our purposes, however, it is in the context of historical applicability that Barth's notion of *das Nichtige* is most vulnerable to legitimate criticism. Within his excursus on Heidegger and Sartre, it is true that Barth locates their respective formulations of evil in the cataclysmic impact of two world wars. 'Heidegger's philosophy is to be found in the First World War in retrospect', whereas Sartre's emerged from the Second [*CD* III/3, 339]. More precisely, Barth seems to believe that, unlike the Enlightenment-optimism which framed the thoughts of Leibniz and Schleiermacher, the wars which Heidegger and Sartre experienced compelled them to take the reality and evil of Nothingness with the utmost seriousness. 'Their thought and expression are determined in and by the considerable though not total upheaval of Western thought and expression occasioned by two world wars' [*CD* III/3, 345]. There is, in other words, an acceptance that history as such can be influential if not determinative in the construction of intellectual discourse. All other criticisms notwithstanding, Barth does at least recognize that traditional paradigms of thought have not and cannot remain unaffected by such traumatic events as the European wars of the early twentieth century and the Nazi era.

On the other hand, nowhere in his thesis on evil does Barth specifically mention the Holocaust. He does argue that no one is capable of 'thinking and speaking as a modern man [*sic*]', or of being understood by contemporaries, if 'the shock experienced and attested by Heidegger and Sartre' does not form part of one's thought-world. His meaning seems to be that, in the 'shock experienced and attested' by the modern world—which, in this context, can only refer to the recent world war—'we men [*sic*] have encountered nothingness' in a profundity previously unknown [*CD* III/3, 345]. This may well be an oblique reference to the *Shoah*. If it is, however, the reference is at the very least vague. Curiously, therefore, Barth seems willing to mention the Second World War in a general sense within the overall context of Nothingness, but not the Holocaust, which was the even more archetypal embodiment of evil.

This hesitation cannot be due either to a lack of knowledge or to a position of denial. As both I and Eberhard Busch have sought to show here and elsewhere, Barth was well aware of the Jewish genocide and throughout the war was actively involved in protesting against it. Davies supplies a more sympathetic reason to account for Barth's silence. 'No one,' he says, 'wrote anything much about the *Shoah* before 1950; it was too soon, and the realization too difficult to grasp.'[63] The chronology of survivor testimony confirms Davies' claim. As Wiesel has said,

> It took me ten years to write…[*Night*]. It was not a coincidence; it was deliberate. I took a vow of silence in 1945, to the effect that I would wait ten years to be sure that what I would say would be true…In the early days, those who were there did not [speak of it]…because they were afraid that no one would believe them.[64]

In other words, that Barth did not mention the Holocaust in his immediate post-war writings cannot in itself be taken as an indication of either indifference or, worse,

---

63 Davies, 21.

64 Elie Wiesel, 'Talking and Writing and Keeping Silent', in F.H. Littell & H.G. Locke (eds), *The German Church Struggle and the Holocaust*, (Detroit: Wayne State University Press, 1974), 274–275.

antisemitism. We may regret that the only possible reference to the Holocaust in his discussion of evil is, at best, thickly veiled. But, given the proximity of the composition of *CD* III/3 to the Holocaust, this obliqueness is arguably understandable.

More problematic is the 'triumph of grace' over evil with which Barth concludes his discussion. According to Barth, the resurrection of Jesus compels us to affirm that Nothingness has been decisively conquered and consigned to the past. 'It is only an echo, a shadow of what it was but is no longer, of what it could do but can do no longer' [*CD* III/3, 367]. Certainly, it still retains a semblance—even a 'dangerous semblance'—of that which it once was. Barth does not rush headlong into an ultimate eschatological conclusion fully realized in the present. That is, Nothingness still has 'standing and significance to the extent that the final revelation of its destruction has not yet taken place...' [*CD* III/3, 367]. We still live *zwischen den Zeiten* of the resurrection and the parousia, in which evil can still deceive us that its power remains unabated. In this deception, however, Nothingness perpetrates its ultimate falsehood, for its previous power and existence are precisely those things that have been destroyed by the redemptive work of Christ. As Von Balthasar has put it, '[Barth] does not take evil any more tragically than God does.'[65]

In the wake of the *Shoah*, however, Barth's argument sounds hollow. 'How, after Auschwitz, can anyone seriously believe that nothingness has lost its dominion...? Does not history refute Barth?'[66] In Berkouwer's opinion, even the testimony of the New Testament is against Barth at this point. In fact, Berkouwer argues that, by so diminishing the objective danger of evil and the demonic in the world, Barth has re-introduced the program of *Entmythologisierung* (de-mythologization) that was so much a part of the nineteenth-century theological outlook from which he wished to escape.[67] We have noticed in respect of Heidegger and Sartre that Barth seems willing to regard the calamity of the two world wars as a unity of events that fractures traditional patterns of thought. What he does not seem prepared to do, however, is acknowledge with Emil Fackenheim that the Holocaust as such renders all *Denkforms* irreparably ruptured.[68] According to Fackenheim, the Holocaust 'forc[es] us to assent to a way of philosophical thought that, immersed in history, is fully exposed to it.'[69] This noetic approach is exactly what Barth wishes to avoid, in order to guard against the danger (as he sees it) of natural theology.

During the years of Nazi rule and the forcible *Gleichschaltung* to which the German Churches and their theologies were exposed, Barth unswervingly argued against the acceptance of general revelation. It was this theological error which led, in his eyes, to the perception of Hitler and the NSDAP as the new revelations of God. Barth was one of the very few churchmen who correctly perceived the basis of the Nazi error. While most opponents of the German regime viewed it purely from an ideological standpoint, Barth realized that Nazism was in fact a heresy, and that its

---

65 Von Balthasar, 231.

66 Davies, 20.

67 Berkouwer, 237, 374–378.

68 'But perhaps *no* thought can exist in the same space as the Holocaust; perhaps *all* thought, to assure its own survival, must be elsewhere.' Fackenheim, *To Mend the World*, 191.

69 Fackenheim, *To Mend the World*, 200.

self-adoption of revelatory status was the essence of its error. Barth's uncompromising rejection of natural theology was thus a critically important stance to take in the years of the *Kirchenkampf*; nonetheless, it seems that it forbade Barth from recognizing the Holocaust as being theologically determinative.

Hence, the answer to the question posed at the beginning of this chapter is, quite clearly, that if the *Shoah* did have an impact upon Barth's post-war theology, it is not at all apparent in his theological construction of evil. For Barth, theological discourse is only legitimately constructed if it is done solely through the lens of christocentric revelation. With this as his paradigmatic frame, Barth thus remains insistent that, since the cross and resurrection of Christ, Nothingness exists merely as a shadow of its former self. When asked by a student in 1962 during his brief visit to Union Theological Seminary, what he would have said had he ever met Adolf Hitler, Barth's answer was both simple and shocking: 'Jesus Christ died for your sins.' Elizabeth Achtemeier has noted '[h]ow irrelevant, how simplistic, how utterly absurd' such a reply seemed to Barth's American audience.[70] In a post-Holocaust world, it is this historical isolationism, not the ambiguous ontology, which represents the greatest weakness of Barth's doctrine.[71]

Conclusion

In this chapter we have considered the changing nature of Karl Barth's theology of revelation. Starting under Herrmann's influence with an existentialized variant of Schleiermacher's theology, we have seen that Barth gradually moved into a dynamic eschatological phase in which the relationship between world-historical events and revelation was a fluctuating one, before culminating in a thoroughgoing rejection of natural theology. In this final phase, Barth was prepared to allow that revelation could indeed become an event—but only as 'God's time'.

The rest of the chapter has posed the question whether or not, in the wake of the Holocaust, Barth renegotiated his understanding of the role of history in theological construction. After such a cataclysmic event, did Barth become more receptive to the suggestion that some history may indeed be determinative for doctrine? In asking this question in respect of Barth's doctrine of evil, the answer has to be a regretful No. Notwithstanding the many fruitful aspects to be found in the concept of *das Nichtige*, its refusal to engage with the most profound actualization of evil in modern times, and the consequently inherent triumph of grace with which the concept is infused, makes it impossible to deny that, at least in this doctrinal context, Barth's *Nein!* remained as vehement as ever. In the next two chapters, the same question will be asked of Barth's theology of Israel to see if, at least here, Barth appropriated some of the lessons of the Holocaust.

---

70 E. Achtemeier, 'Relevant Remembering', in McKim, 110.

71 For exploration of the potential utility ingredient to Barth's concept of *das Nichtige*, notwithstanding its lack of historical engagement, see M.R. Lindsay, '"Nothingness" Revisited: Karl Barth's doctrine of radical evil in the wake of the Holocaust', in *Colloquium*, vol.34, no.1 (2002), 3–19.

Postscript

A final word needs to be said at this point regarding my own attitude toward natural theology. As I have tried to make clear in this chapter, I do not see significant evidence of Barth having incorporated the historical events of the Holocaust into his understanding of radical evil. Not surprisingly, this has been viewed by many as a serious lacuna in Barth's overall contribution to twentieth-century theology. It is evident that Barth is in no doubt of the 'evilness' of evil—but he explores this in isolation from the most profound realization of evil in modern times.

Having said this, though, I cannot help but feel that Barth's position remains valid as a critical safeguard against the arbitrary reading of revelation off the face of history. It should be remembered that it was precisely this arbitrariness that enabled German popular opinion after the defeat of 1918 to see in the German *Volkstum* a necessary complement to Christianity, and later the *Deutsche Christen Bewegung* to see in Hitler the new revelation of God. We forget this at our peril. Once divine revelation is viewed from the perspective of the λόγος ἄσαρκος, or 'Logos in itself' [*CD* IV/1, 52]—once, in other words, we remove from revelation its christological content—we run the very real danger of allowing revelation to attach itself to anything we so desire. As James Torrance has argued,

> today we witness the demand for certain forms of indigenous theology…which [want] to detach 'the Christ' from Jesus Christ, and then attach the idea to an indigenous culture and traditional spirituality.

Torrance understands that 'this, of course, can be motivated by the recognition that we in the West have too often detached Jesus Christ from his roots in Israel and created…a Gentile Christ…'[72] Nonetheless, the danger is that 'when such ideas are detached from the gospel of the incarnation and attached to ourselves, they can become the basis of an ideology, a political agenda in terms of which everything else is interpreted.'[73]

There is a related methodological question, too. If revelation *can* be read off the face of history, does that mean that it *has* to be? And if not, what are the criteria for deciding whether what one is observing is or is not revelational? To put it in other words, if natural theology is not an acceptable option, is there nonetheless a way in which the uniquely and undeniably theological significance of the Holocaust can still be incorporated into Christian theological discourse? A number of possibilities suggest themselves. From the Barthian perspective, his so-called 'doctrine of lights' [*CD* IV/3.1], at which we will look briefly in Chapter Five, is of potential utility.

Another possibility is Dietrich Ritschl's concept of 'rediscovery'. In Ritschl's opinion, it is only rarely that the words of Scripture make a direct impact that then translates into action. More commonly, he argues, there is a 'rediscovery' or verification of scriptural truth through a 'process of inductive knowledge by which a present problem area or task is connected with elements latent in the memory of

---

72 J.B. Torrance, *Worship, Community, and the Triune God of Grace*, (Carlisle: The Paternoster Press, 1996), 104.

73 J.B. Torrance, 102.

the church.'[74] For example, dispute and reconciliation can be the rediscovery of the prodigal son story. Likewise, hatred, envy and greed can lead, negatively, to a rediscovery of a central message of the Hebrew Scriptures, simply because they deny so clearly the key concerns of the *Tanakh*. Ritschl terms such rediscoveries, embedded as they are within the concreteness of practical life, the 'occasions of revelation'. Whether or not the Holocaust could fit this paradigm is an open question, but one that is most certainly worth pursuing.

Finally, there is, of course, a crucial interfaith perspective to this issue. All religions believe that their own teachings are predicated upon their own reception of divine revelation. Some assume an exclusivist position on this, and claim that *only* in their particular religion is the revelation of God *truly* known. Christianity has traditionally understood itself in this way. Pertinent to this book, then, is the question whether or not Barth's concept of revelation precludes the possibility of genuine revelation within Israel, and to that extent genuine dialogue *with* Jews?

I have endeavoured to show in *Covenanted Solidarity* that, in Barth's mind, christologically-circumscribed revelation does not preclude but indeed necessitates Jewish–Christian unity. It is true that for Barth the only mode of the Word of God that can, without qualification, be identified with God's revelation is Jesus Christ [*CD* I/1, 115–117]. Nonetheless, the unity of the Hebrew and Christian Scriptures are attestations of that one Word of God and, 'to the extent that the Bible really attests revelation it is no less the Word of God than revelation itself' [*CD* I/1, 121]. In fact, 'it is only in this unity that the biblical witness is the witness of divine revelation' [*CD* I/2, 482].

> [It] is not a matter of an historical relation between two religions ['Christianity' and 'Judaism'], nor yet of one that can be described by the concepts of 'kinship' or of 'homogeneity', but of unity in revelation in both cases which connects the two so-called religions. [*CD* I/2, 79]

Consequently, Barth is able to affirm that the Old and New Testaments are held together by the revealed name of God, Yahweh-Kyrios, and thus that God really was revealed to and through Israel.[75]

According to Kendall Soulen, this formulation presents a critically important insight, and one that potentially undermines the supersessionist agenda that has, as we saw in the Introduction, typically funded traditional trinitarian theology. For Barth, argues Soulen,

> YHWH, the God of Israel, is not an item that can be treated as peripheral or optional... On the contrary, God's identity as YHWH is *central and indispensable* for the whole of trinitarian reflection...Taken seriously, Barth's [thesis] recognizes that God's identity as the God of Israel possesses *criteriological significance*...[76]

---

74 Ritschl, 76.

75 For a more detailed exploration of this theme, see my *Covenanted Solidarity*, ch.5, especially 185–191.

76 Soulen, 'YHWH the Triune God', 35.

Crucially, therefore, Barth's insistence that the name of God that is made known through revelation—Yahweh-Kyrios—is 'sufficiently attested only by the simultaneous witness of the canon *as a whole*.'[77]

This is not to say that Barth's formulation here is without its problems. Soulen, for example, argues that the name of God's identity contains within itself the roots of its own insufficiency. That is, that the name Yahweh is determined as to its content by the title Kyrios, and thus that Kyrios is an ultimately more complete revelation of the being and nature of God.[78] To put it slightly differently, Barth regards the revelation attested in the Old Testament as genuine *to the extent that* it points toward Jesus Christ.

This is, of course, highly problematic for the purpose of Jewish–Christian relations. I would suggest, however, that there is no need to go quite as far as Barth does; that the unity of the Testaments that is guaranteed by the name Yahweh-Kyrios holds true even without relegating the Hebrew Scriptures to the status of 'expectation'. That is to say, that it is possible—*even for the Christian*—to honour the reality of the revelation in the Old Testament *in and of itself*. Indeed, I would argue that Barth's logic actually entails such a conclusion. According to Barth's Göttingen cycle of dogmatics, 'The content of revelation is God alone, wholly God, God himself' [*GD*, 87]. Either, says Barth, 'God speaks, or he does not.'

> God is not just half revealed or partly revealed, so that another part of his being or attributes or acts will have to remain hidden or will have to be imparted in some other way than by revelation…Revelation is either the whole revelation of God or it is not revelation. [*GD*, 91–93]

If, then, God is revealed at all in the Old Testament, he is revealed completely, quite apart from the revelation attested in the New Testament. This, it seems to me, is a quite defensible basis on which Jews and Christians can begin to dialogue.

---

77 Soulen, 'YHWH the Triune God', 37.
78 Soulen, 'YHWH the Triune God', 37

Chapter Four

Karl Barth and the State of Israel: Between theology and politics

It is a quirk of Barth scholarship that, while many commentators have unquestioningly accepted the received 'wisdom' that Barth espoused an economic (although not punitive) supersessionism that was little short of outright antisemitism, he is nonetheless credited with having been in his later years an avowed champion of the State of Israel. In Barth's view, the restoration of the Jews to their homeland was 'like seeing an ancient map come alive…[It was] the burst[ing] forth of a living nation and people, at once ancient and new…'[1] Even this joyful witnessing of the Jews' re-establishment, though, does not pass without criticism. In Katherine Sonderegger's view, Barth's support for the Israeli nation is only a 'reluctant admiration'. Given Barth's 'deep anti-Judaism', it is a 'surprising' admiration that is borne, not out of genuine affection, but rather out of Barth's dogmatic presuppositions, according to which the Jews are fated to stand as silent witnesses, both to their unbelief and to God's 'free and justifying grace' that triumphs even in spite of Jewish disobedience.

To put it in other words, Sonderegger's argument is that the re-emergence of the State of Israel after the horrors of the Holocaust supplies yet more evidence for Barth to bolster his belief that the Jews exist merely as a 'riddle', explicable only with reference to God's sovereignty and revelation.[2] But is this really Barth's own view? Can §49.3 of the *Church Dogmatics* really only be read in such a way? Or, and in spite of Barth's seeming reluctance to acknowledge the theological significance of the *Shoah*, at which we looked in the last chapter, is it possible to interpret Barth's response to the creation of Israel in a more positive light? Indeed, in his search to explain the foundation of Israel, do we in fact see at last a concession to the legitimacy of natural theology? These are the questions with which this chapter will be concerned.

Out of the Ashes: The 1948 (re-)creation of Israel

On 14 May 1948, David Ben Gurion read out the Scroll of Independence in the Tel Aviv museum, thereby proclaiming the establishment of the State of Israel. The proclamation of statehood was greeted enthusiastically by both the United States and the Soviet Union, although Paul Johnson has noted that Israel's post-war emergence

---

1   K. Sonderegger, 'The Cup of Wrath.' Sermon delivered at the Virginia Theological Seminary, 8 April 2003.

2   Sonderegger, *That Jesus Christ Was Born a Jew*, 135, 138, 156, 158–159.

from British authority was more a matter of luck than of good management by the Zionists. Israel, he says, 'slipped into existence through a fortuitous window in history...'[3]

It is a matter of significant debate how the 1948 creation of Israel should be interpreted historically. Johnson speaks for many when he states that Israel came into being as 'the consequence of Jewish sufferings' during the Holocaust.[4] It arose, phoenix-like, from the smouldering ashes of the death camps. Or, in religious rather than mythological terms, Israel's re-birth was a 'resurrection', after the 'crucifixion' of the Jews in Auschwitz.[5] Conversely, Richard Rubenstein speaks for those who refuse to endorse a causative link between the two. The horrors of the *Shoah* and the events surrounding the establishment of Israel in 1948 must, argues Rubenstein, be kept (at least theologically) independent of one another. If they are not, one runs the risk of retrospectively infusing the Holocaust with positive significance. That is, to employ the theological terminology of crucifixion and resurrection is to imply that the Holocaust was somehow necessary before the resurrection-event of 1948 could take place. Rubenstein's argument is compelling. Whatever flaws his historiography may entail—at the level of empirical causation, it is hard to separate Auschwitz and Israel entirely—one can certainly sympathize with his insistence that the *Shoah* lacked any redeeming qualities.[6]

In more specifically theological language, David Fox Samuel has affirmed that the 'children of Israel...have a deep emotional attachment to a particular *land* that we also call Israel.' And, while the land of Israel is far older than the present-day geopolitical nation-state,

---

3   P. Johnson, *A History of the Jews*, (London: Orion, 1993), 526.

4   Johnson, 519.

5   See for example, F.H. Littell, 'Christian Antisemitism and the Holocaust', in R.L. Braham (ed.), *Perspectives on the Holocaust*, (Boston: Kluwer-Nijhoff Publishing, 1983), 44. For examples of Jewish theologians who have perceived a religious, even covenantal, link between the Holocaust and the State of Israel, see Emil Fackenheim and Eliezer Berkovits. According to Fackenheim, the State of Israel is the *Tikkun*, the 'healing' that comes after the rupture of the Holocaust. Fackenheim, 312–313. Berkovits, meanwhile, interprets Israel as contemporary revelation. 'If at Auschwitz...we have witnessed "The Hiding Face of God", in the rebirth of the State of Israel and its success "we have seen a smile on the face of God."' E. Berkovits, *Faith After the Holocaust*, (New York, 1973), 156. Cited in S. Katz, *Post-Holocaust Dialogues: Critical Studies in Modern Jewish Thought*, (New York: New York University Press, 1983), 167.

6   There is, surprisingly enough, a body of Jewish though, articulated most clearly by Ignaz Maybaum, that in fact *does* see some positive significance in the Holocaust. According to Maybaum, the Holocaust should be viewed through the paradigm of vicarious atonement. Israel has a global mission in bringing the gentile nations to God. But, in order to do so, Israel has to 'speak' in a language that the non-Jewish nations will understand. This language, says Maybaum, is one in which 'progress requires and is mediated through death and destruction... To engage the nations God must speak in the tones of *Churban*, destruction, for this is the only vocabulary that they are attuned to, the only expression to which they will respond.' Thus, events of *Churban*, such as the Holocaust, are revelatory because they 'bring gentiles to God...[and signal] the end of one epoch and the beginning of another, better era in Jewish and world annals.' See Katz, 157–158.

[in] the light of a history marked by persecution and genocide, the existence of an independent Jewish state, also called Israel, has made the connection to both the land and the state an integral part of what it means for contemporary Jews to be Israel.[7]

Clearly, then, irrespective of whether it is granted positive or negative significance, there is a general tendency within Jewish post-Holocaust thought to at least make the connection between land and religion.

What, though, of Christian theological and ecclesiastical responses to the foundation of the Israeli State? While Markus Barth has insisted that the State of Israel has given Judaism 'a form which is to be affirmed and supported by the church', in reality Christian responses have been uncertain and ambiguous.[8] According to the Scottish theologian David Torrance, that Israel 'has emerged in the Land of Promise...full of hope' and 'at the heart of world politics' is 'a remarkable testimony to the Hand of God at work in his world.'[9] Another of the Torrance brothers, Thomas, argues in a similar vein. For him, the 'establishment of the new State of Israel...is surely the most significant sign given by God in his providential dealings with his covenanted People since...AD 70.'[10]

On the other hand, however, the Anglican Bishop of Oxford Richard Harries laments the fact that formal Church responses have been at best ambivalent and tardy.[11] Conway reminds us that 'many Jewish observers have been sharply critical of the churches' numerous utterances about the State of Israel'[12]—and at times, for good reason. Just weeks before Ben Gurion's formal announcement of Israel's independent statehood, for example, the *United Church Observer* in Canada urged that 'For the sake of the world, the Jews should renounce their [fanatical] claims for an immediate sovereign state', on the basis that it would be 'contrary to history.'[13] Then, just three months after the foundation, the World Council of Churches (WCC) met in Amsterdam for its inaugural assembly. Although antisemitism itself was condemned by the Council, the 'establishment of the state "Israel" add[ed] a political dimension to the Christian approach to the Jews and threatened[ed] to complicate antisemitism with political fears and enmities.' So vexing was the issue that the WCC delegates refused 'to express a judgment.'[14] As Allan Brockway has

7   D.F. Samuel, Israel, Judaism, and Christianity', in T. Frymer-Kensky, D. Novak, P. Ochs, D.F. Samuel & M.A. Signer (eds), *Christianity in Jewish Terms*, (Boulder, CO: Westview Press, 2000), 160.

8   M. Barth, *The People of God*, (Sheffield: JSOT Press, 1983), 72.

9   D.W. Torrance, 'Israel Today, in the Light of God's Word', in D.W. Torrance (ed.), *The Witness of the Jews to God*, (Edinburgh: The Handsel Press, 1982), 105.

10   T.F. Torrance, 'The Divine Vocation and Destiny of Israel in World History', in D.W. Torrance, 94.

11   Harries, 141.

12   Conway, 'The Changes in Recent Decades in the Churches' Doctrine', 549.

13   *United Church Observer*, 10 [3], (1948–49), 4. Significantly, Canada itself withheld *de facto* recognition of Israel until December 1948 and abstained from the first formal vote to admit Israel to the UN. Similarly, the Roman Catholic Church in Quebec was openly hostile to the establishment of the Israeli State.

14   Cited in Harries, 140–141.

said, the WCC 'was confused about what to say.'[15] The situation was similar at both the second and third assemblies. When the WCC's Faith and Order Commission produced a more theologically-based report on the relationship between Christians and Jews in 1968, it too was flummoxed. The creation of Israel was, the report affirmed, 'of tremendous importance for the great majority of Jews', but it 'has also brought suffering and injustice to the Arab people', and thus the Commission was again unable and unwilling to present a consensual opinion.[16]

There are a number of reasons for this uncertainty. At one level, the successful emergence of a Jewish state in Israel's traditional homeland makes a mockery of the age-old Christian assumption that the Jews' global dispersion—in effect, their expulsion from their own land—signifies their punishment at the hand of God. At an entirely more pragmatic level, many of the Christian missionary societies that were active in the Middle East were concerned that any alignment with the new Israeli State would jeopardize their progress among the Arab nations. As a result, such societies were deeply reluctant 'to recognise the validity of [Israel], let alone foster any idea that the restoration of Israel could be a source of theological renewal for Christianity.'[17]

Not surprisingly, with the notable exception of the so-called 'Religious Right' in the USA,[18] most mainstream Churches have struggled to marry an endorsement of Israel's statehood as a theological *datum* with the undeniably repressive policies that Israel has enacted against Palestinian co-habitants and neighbours. In consequence, and alongside a wariness of the naïve literalism of fundamentalist dispensationalism, these Churches have resisted granting theological importance to the Israeli State. There is a fear that to do so would be seen as a *de facto* endorsement of Israel's political and military policies. Thus, at the 1987 meeting of the Anglican Consultative Council in Singapore, it was agreed that Israel as a member state of the United Nations had a political right to exist, but there was a vehement rejection of 'the interpretation of Holy Scripture which affirms a special place for the present State of Israel...'[19] In the same year, the General Assembly of the Presbyterian Church of the United States presented a report on the 'Theological Understanding of the Relationship Between Christians and Jews'. Notwithstanding its 'willingness to investigate the continuing significance of the promise of "land"...', the Assembly nonetheless asserted that 'The State of Israel is a geopolitical entity and is not to be validated theologically.'[20]

---

15 A. Brockway, 'The Churches in the Search for Middle East Peace', *Christian Social Action*, (1996).

16 Cited in Harries, 141.

17 Conway, 'The Changes in Recent Decades in the Churches' Doctrine', 550.

18 The 'Religious Right' is an ambiguous (and not entirely accurate) umbrella term for the various conservative evangelical lobby groups in the USA, such as Jerry Falwell's Moral Majority (now, the Moral Majority Coalition), James Dobson's Focus on the Family, and Pat Robertson's Christian Coalition of America. Many of these organizations adopt a specifically pro-Israel political position and actively lobby against Palestinian self-determination.

19 Resolutions of the Anglican Consultative Council (ACC)-7. Res.25b,c (1987).

20 'A Theological Understanding of the Relationship Between Christians and Jews.' Report of the Council on Theology and Culture of the Presbyterian Church of the United

Such attitudes have been interpreted by many Jews to indicate that Christianity is still simply unable to grasp the inseparability within Judaism of religion and place. Very few European Churches have followed in the footsteps of the Netherlands Reform Church which, in 1970, took the wholly surprising view that 'if the election of the people [Israel] and the promises connected with it remain valid, it follows that the tie between the people and the land also remains by the grace of God.'[21]

'The relationship of covenant to land,' says Geoffrey Wigoder, 'is as much outside the Christian experience as the centrality of Jesus in the mystery of the triune God is outside the Jewish experience.'[22] Or, as Mordecai Waxman puts it, there is for many Churches 'a lurking assumption that…Israel is actually a political rather than a theological issue…[T]he niggling statement "Israel has a right to exist"…is the reluctant admission of foreign office bureaucrats, not churchmen.'[23]

But what of Barth's response? How did he interpret the creation of Israel, both theologically and politically? Coincidentally, at the very time that Ben Gurion was proclaiming Israel's independence, Barth was busy with another political 'hot potato'. In late March of 1948, Barth made his second visit to Hungary (the first had been made almost exactly ten years earlier) at the invitation of the Hungarian Reformed Church, to deliver a series of public lectures and sermons. In his third of the series, 'Christliche Gemeinde im Wechsel der Staatsordnungen', which he delivered in Budapest and Sarospatak, Barth noted with pleasure that the Hungarian Church seemed to be maintaining the right balance between opposition to and cooperation with the new Communist regime.[24] Barth's comments provoked a storm of controversy in Switzerland and elsewhere, with Barth's old sparring-partner, Emil Brunner, accusing Barth of harbouring pro-Communist sympathies. Brunner simply could not grasp why Barth, who had been so vehemently opposed to Nazism, was not similarly outspoken against Communism. The debates that followed raged for some months—indeed for years, as the 1956 Hungarian crisis provoked the American theologian Reinhold Niebuhr to again raise the issue of Barth's alleged 'crypto-communism'.[25]

While Cold War tensions were the public face of Barth's political activism at this time, they were not the only events of global significance to be occupying Barth's mind. As concerned as he was to find the appropriate response to the ideological battle between East and West, Barth was just as concerned with formulating the right political and theological response to the 1948 creation of Israel. Not surprisingly, Barth's theological response to Israel's declaration of independence formed the basis of his political response, and it was in his 'Doctrine of Creation' that he ventured an initial reaction.

States, and presented to the 199th General Assembly in Biloxi, Missouri (1987), 4, 14.

21 General Synod of the Netherlands Reform Church, 1970. Cited in Harries, 148.

22 G. Wigoder, *Jewish–Christian Relations since the Second World War*, (Manchester University Press, 1988), 105. Cited in Harries, 142.

23 Cited in Harries, 148.

24 K. Barth, 'Christliche Gemeinde im Wechsel der Staatsordnungen', in *Against the Stream*, 77–93.

25 K. Barth, *Brief an einen Pfarrer in der DDR*, (Evangelischer Verlag, 1958), 6. Cited in Busch, *Karl Barth*, 427.

The Creation of Israel in 'The Doctrine of Creation'

By intriguing coincidence, Barth commenced work on *CD* III/3 in the summer of 1948. At the very time that he was beginning his discussion of divine providence, with which the third part-volume of his 'Doctrine of Creation' is essentially concerned, the Jewish people were being re-established on their traditional land. As we shall come to see, Barth felt himself compelled to interpret the foundation of Israel as a temporal sign of God's providential care.

Before being able fully to appreciate what Barth says about Israel in his section on 'The Divine Ruling' (§49.3), it is therefore extremely useful to look first at how he understands the concept of providence itself.[26] Barth begins by noting that the doctrine of *de providentia Dei* 'requires clarification' [*CD* III/3, 3]. Of course, if this was true in 1948, it is even more so now; not surprisingly, the idea that God sustains and cares for the created world has come under severe attack, not only now from science,[27] but arguably even more so from the genocidal history of the past century that has fundamentally challenged the notion of an interventionist God.

Barth's response to this need for clarification is instructive. He argues that providence is in fact faith in Christ, but that this recognition has been lost and replaced with a simplistic correlation between providence and a generalized theism. Such a correlation has 'inevitably proved to be inadequate…in face of…the external and internal catastrophes of the 19th and 20th centuries.' With the exception of the 1755 Lisbon earthquake, Barth does not identify what these catastrophes are that he has in mind, nor does he explain the difference between an 'internal' and an 'external' catastrophe. Yet we do get a certain clue: with a sombre glance back at recent German history, Barth notes quite rightly that 'providence' was 'a favourite [word] on the lips of Adolf Hitler' [*CD* III/3, 33].[28] In other words Barth, for whom

---

26 For a brief but very good overview of Barth's doctrine of providence, see C. Schröder, ' "I See Something You Don't See": Karl Barth's Doctrine of Providence', and the 'Response' by R.C. Zachman, in Hunsinger, *For the Sake of the World*, 115–142.

27 For an excellent discussion of the recent history of the 'Science vs Theology' debate, see R.J. Russell & K. Wegter-McNelly, 'Science', in G. Jones (ed.), *The Blackwell Companion to Modern Theology*, (Oxford: Blackwell, 2004), 512–533.

28 Hitler was obsessed with the notion of his own, and Germany's, destiny and typically spoke of it in religious terms. Among many similar examples, Hitler is reported to have stated that 'Those who see in National Socialism nothing more than a political movement know scarcely anything of it. It is more even than a religion; it is the will to create mankind anew.' Adolf Hitler, cited in H. Rauschning *Hitler Speaks*, (London: Thornton Butterworth, 1940), 241–242. Similarly, the Youth Leader of the German Reich, Baldur von Schirach, said that Hitler indoctrinated Germany's youth with 'religious faith in Hitler as the New Messiah.' Also, Robert Ley (German Labour Front) claimed in 1937 that 'God has sent us Adolf Hitler', while Siegfried Leffler (co-founder of the Thüringer Deutsche Christen) proclaimed Hitler as the 'Saviour whom God sent.' See P. Viereck, *Metapolitics: The Roots of the Nazi Mind*, (New York: Capricorn Books, 1965), 287–289. Significantly, it was Dietrich Bonhoeffer who was the first theologian to publicly recognize (and condemn) the religious hubris of Nazism. In his radio address of 1 February 1933, 'Der Führer und der einzelne in der jungen Generation', Bonhoeffer decried the illegitimate transformation of the 'matter-of-fact idea of political authority' into 'the political, messianic concept of Leader (*Führer*) as we know it today.' See *GS* II, 32.

the National Socialist appropriation of Christian doctrine was all too familiar ground, has consciously linked the widespread failure to understand the essential substance of providence, to the horrors of Nazism by which the doctrine seems to have been so clearly discredited. As far as Barth is thus concerned, it is hardly surprising that the generally accepted idea of providence is unable to cope with the traumas of Nazism, the Second World War and (although he does not explicitly say it) the Holocaust, as it lacks its essential christological foundation.

Nonetheless, Barth is keen to affirm what, for many then and for even more now, was and is an anachronistic doctrine. For him, providence means that 'in every respect and in its whole span [the history of the created being] proceeds under the fatherly care of God...' [*CD* III/3, 3].[29] Somewhat uncomfortably, Barth is as a result logically compelled to accept that 'whatever may take place in the history of the creature' occurs, in some or other sense, under the direct lordship of God. In so saying, Barth falls foul of the dilemma posed by Rubenstein, that one can *either* accept that God was the ultimate Author of Auschwitz, *or* that God is not the omnipotent and beneficent Lord depicted in the Hebrew and Christian Scriptures. Significantly, even Rubenstein has accepted that this affirmation of God's sovereignty, even and especially in the midst of trauma, is 'in harmony with Scripture' and is essentially no different to anything 'spoken by the prophets and rabbis in the past.'[30] Barth does not, of course, accept the Rubensteinian solution of avoiding the either/or dilemma by rejecting the biblical image of God. He does, however, at least seem to recognize the general difficulty that this doctrine entails; that the lordship of God is not at all transparently evident, and that in very many situations and 'to all appearances we have to do only with...the works of caprice and...folly' [*CD* III/3, 13, 43–44]. In such situations, divine providence takes the form of *Hester Panim*, the 'hidden face of God.'

What this means for Barth's comprehension of evil and theodicy is, as we saw in Chapter Two, explored under the rubric of *das Nichtige*, in §50 of *CD* III/3. In our discussion of Nothingness, we noticed that Barth is reluctant to address the *Shoah* and seems unable, or unwilling, to see in it an historical example of radical evil. And yet, as we shall see, Barth seems to take a different approach in regard to the events of 1948. In contrast to his reticence to incorporate the Holocaust into his doctrine of evil, Barth does discuss in great detail the establishment of Israel as the positive pole of God's commitment to humanity. As we continue, we shall ask whether this represents a softening of Barth's attitude toward natural theology.

---

29 Barth here goes only part of the way with the older dogmaticians. The act of creation is 'a once-for-all act, not repeated or repeatable.' There are no 'further acts of creation... Providence guarantees and confirms the work of creation...[but] this does not mean, however, that [God] continually creates it afresh' [*CD* III/3, 6]. In contrast, J.H. Heidegger argues that 'Preservation is not an act distinct from creation but is continued creation.' Similarly, Braun says that God's providence is identical with the 'effective volition of God'. So, 'In respect of God the same action is creation *and* providence...' See J.H. Heidegger, *Corpus Theologiae*, (Zurich, 1700), VII, 22; J. Braun, *Doctrina Foederumsive Systema Theologiae didacticae et elencticae*, (Amsterdam, 1688), I, ii, 12, 1. Both in H. Heppe, *Reformed Dogmatics*, trans. G.T. Thomson, (London: Allen & Unwin, 1950), 251.

30 Rubenstein, 170.

In answering this question, it is important to note at the outset that this divine commitment is not, for Barth, intrinsic to the existence of humanity as such, but is rather a function of the covenant of grace of which God is and remains the free author. So, when Barth says of (biblical and post-biblical) Israel that the security of its creaturely existence is located *only* in God's faithful preservation of the covenant [*CD* III/3, 84], he is not singling Israel out for special treatment but, on the contrary, is using Israel as a cipher by which he makes the same point about *all* humanity. Thus, that Barth finds it necessary to affirm God's lordship over 'whatever may take place' in world history, is grounded in his belief that providence is the historical actualization of the covenantal reality that God is *for us*.

This inextricable connection between providence and the revelation of gracious election through Jesus Christ is, naturally enough, lacking in Jewish theology. Hence, Barth speaks, for example, of the 'semi-biblical religion of post-Christian Judaism' that believes only in a content-less and abstract knowledge of the history of salvation, and of the God by whom this history is in fact authored. The 'devout Jew', according to Barth's framework of understanding, can therefore only ever enjoy an 'unfulfilled' belief in the *principle* of God's lordship, an 'approximating' belief which inevitably engenders 'anxious and hypercritical concern' as to the reality and beneficence of that lordship, in contrast to (the Christian's) 'childlike confidence' [*CD* III/3, 28].

There is no doubt that this type of language seems at the very least to be patronizing and derogatory. And perhaps it is. But a more even-handed reading must recognize that this christological deficiency which Barth finds in Judaism's theology of providence is precisely what he also finds to be lacking in the earlier Reformed tradition and is the very reason why the doctrine itself needs clarifying. If he is critical of the Jewish misunderstanding of providence, he is even more severe with his own theological forebears. The 'older Protestant theology was guilty of an almost total failure' to perceive the essence of providence, says Barth. The Lutheran and Reformed dogmaticians of the sixteenth and seventeenth centuries understood the doctrine purely as an 'empty shell', dictated by the theological abstractions of omnipotence and omniscience, without any christological reference.[31] Not even in Calvin, laments Barth, do we find 'a single pointer…that [he] understands the doctrine of providence wholly on the basis of the revelation of God in Jesus Christ' [*CD* III/3, 30–31]. But why is this basis of christological revelation so vital? Because the power and purpose of God's preservation of humanity finds its locus in the Person of Jesus Christ. Taking as his starting-point the doxology of Rom.11:36— ὅτι ἐξ αὐτοῦ καὶ δι' αὐτοῦ καὶ εἰς αὐτὸν τὰ πάντα —Barth states the following

> The creature has to be preserved, and is in fact preserved, because this particular will of God has to be done, and is in fact done, both in heaven and on earth, because Jesus Christ is at the right hand of the Father and is our Advocate. It is He who represents our right to existence…It is He who is the divine basis of the preservation and continuance of that existence. For its preservation is for His sake. It is the outflowing, the presupposition and

---

31 In Heinrich Heppe's summary of Reformed dogmatics, which proved so useful to Barth as he began his first professorial appointment in Göttingen in 1924, Jesus Christ is mentioned only once by name in the entire section on Providence. See Heppe, ch.XII.

the consequence of the grace which God gave to the creaturely world in His Son, and it takes place in order that in the creaturely world God may be glorified in and through His Son...It takes place as and because God the Father is (in His Son) *for* the creature. [*CD* III/3, 58–59]

Thus, the purpose of God's providential care for humanity lies in the fact that it is this creature that has been 'chosen, willed, and posited by God' to be the 'theatre of the covenant' [*CD* III/1, 99]. Humanity exists because it has been elected *to be*, in stark contrast to the non-willed reality of *das Nichtige*, which exists as that which God has precisely *not* elected. God does not just create and preserve humankind, but remains *with* (and to that extent, *for*) us. Moreover, of course, God's 'being with and for' humanity is not an abstract notion of accompaniment. Despite following Cocceius' formula of *nutus voluntatis in Deo...comitatur operationem creaturae*, which Barth acknowledges to be 'a very general...and for that reason most hazardous' concept, he immediately rejects the suggestion that God's accompaniment is weak, indifferent or passive [*CD* III/3, 91]. On the contrary, the activity of God through which humanity is accompanied by God's providential care (the old doctrine of *concursus*), is God's eternal love. Barth's presupposition regarding divine providence is therefore founded upon the notion of God being eternally and lovingly with and for humanity. It is vital that this be kept in mind as we turn now to the third aspect of *de providentia Dei*, the divine ruling, in which Barth attends to the question of Israel.

De Gubernatione and the King of Israel

Barth states at the outset of §49.3 that the sphere of the divine ruling, *de gubernatione*, is 'decisive for the whole doctrine of the divine providence' [*CD* III/3, 154]. That his longest discussion of Israel within 'The Doctrine of Creation' occurs within this pivotal section suggests that Israel itself occupies a central place within his thinking. Of course, that Israel may occupy a central place in this doctrine is not necessarily an indication that Israel or the Jewish people are accorded a positive status in Barth's thought. Indeed, it is precisely here that Barth comes closest to disembodying Jews and depicting them through the faceless cipher of an 'Israel-concept'. As Joseph Mangina has recently put it,

> the irony of Barth's account of Israel is that while he in one sense accords it the highest possible dignity—it is the irrevocably elect people of God—he fails to honour the material, embodied existence of the Jewish people in history.[32]

He runs the risk, in other words, of portraying Jews as little more than constitutive elements of a paradigmatic construct. But is this what he intends? Keeping in mind his contention that the character of the divine ruling is not God's exercise of raw power for its own sake but is, on the contrary, the ruling of a *Father* [*CD* III/3, 155],

---

32 J. Mangina, *Karl Barth: Theologian of Christian Witness*, (Aldershot: Ashgate, 2004), 185.

a close reading of §49.3 suggests that Barth's intent in fact lies in the direction of a far more sympathetic understanding.[33]

According to Barth, the subject of the *gubernatio*, God the Father, is none other than the King of Israel. Moreover, this ruling Father is the King of Israel as much in the New Testament as in the Old. He is 'the same Lord *of the same covenant*' [*CD* III/3, 176, 179]. As Barth puts it,

> The King of Israel is the King of the world. It is His will that is done in the ruling of all creaturely occurrence. It is He who is the Lord over it…The fact that it concerns Him, the King of Israel, is what distinguishes…the divine ruling from an empty idea, or from the uncertain and in any case unchristian idea of the power and activity of a supreme being. If it concerns the King of Israel, we are on solid ground and under sure leadership…To put it another way: The King of Israel is the One who according to the witness of the Old and New Testaments spoke the 'I am', and in speaking it actualised it for seeing eyes and hearing ears by acts of power within the created cosmos and human history. [*CD* III/3, 176–177]

Even Katherine Sonderegger accepts that this insistence on covenantal solidarity precludes Barth's theology of Israel from being a straightforwardly 'supersessionist decree.'[34] How, though, does the Father-King in fact rule Israel?

Barth begins his discussion of the divine ruling by stating three general principles. First, God rules alone and is, in consequence, the goal, the *telos*, to which His rule directs not only humanity but the entirety of creation [*CD* III/3, 158–159]. Barth takes this to mean that God is not imprisoned by the necessities or logic of the 'cosmic processes' [*CD* III/3, 160–161].

> God's rule is not as it were identical with the logic with which natural events are seen to occur according to the norm of what we call natural laws, although no doubt it is present in and by this logic…Nor is it identical with the logic of world-historical, political or economic developments and relationships, although there certainly are such things, and God's overruling is certainly present in and by them. A clear perception of necessity in world-occurrence does not mean that God has to be explained or approached as though He were so tied to this necessity that He is virtually its prisoner. God rules in and by this necessity, but He also goes His own way through it. [*CD* III/3, 160–161]

For this reason, says Barth, God 'laughs at all our attempts to see His rule with the eye of human reason' [*CD* III/3, 160]. Whatever else Barth might say about the State of Israel, then, his understanding of God's sole sovereignty over world-historical occurrence must mean that the State's foundation in 1948 can in the end only be explained with reference to God's rule.

---

33 In one of his later English-speaking colloquia, Barth confessed that he did not, in retrospect, like the way in which he had sought to describe the character of 'God the Father' in *CD* I/1, §10. A better description would have given greater emphasis to the *love* of God the Father. As it stands, says Barth, in §10 'the notion of fatherhood is cold; it does not give the impression of the warm love of the Father.' See J.D. Godsey (ed.), *Karl Barth's Table Talk*, Scottish Journal of Theology Occasional Papers No.10, (Edinburgh & London: Oliver & Boyd, 1963), 51.

34 Sonderegger, *That Jesus Christ Was Born a Jew*, 133.

Barth's second general point is that God rules by establishing order, where order means the 'continuing operation by which an occurrence in time takes place in accordance with a definite plan, and is determined and formed and directed through constantly changing situations and stages' [*CD* III/3, 164]. Although Barth extrapolates from this the argument that God's ordering of humanity's activity is also therefore its controlling, he is careful not to imply that humanity's activity is consequently not free. Indeed, specifically within God's ordering, a sphere is made in which we can work freely and independently, with the dignity of created autonomy—albeit that this activity is nonetheless controlled by God 'in its freedom no less than its necessity' [*CD* III/3, 165].

> [The creature] does use this freedom. It is active at every moment. But in every moment it uses this freedom on the basis of the particular divine permission to do so. It works always within the framework and the limits of this permission. There can be no question of a compulsion laid upon it. But also there can be no question of an activity apart from this divine permission…God controls, but in doing so He orders. Hence we see that in so far as God determines all creaturely activity and its effects, it is settled that the individual actions which go to make up world history are at least co-ordinated actions, co-ordinated, that is, by His all-embracing ordination. [*CD* III/3, 166–167]

The third general point Barth makes before turning to the 'material content' of the divine ruling arises from the objection to the common goal to which creaturely (human) activity is directed. It could, in other words, be assumed that Barth's formulation of God's rule naturally implies a creaturely uniformity; that the common goal of human activity erases the historic and visible particularities of the different human groupings. But this is not what Barth wishes to suggest. In his *Ethics*, he had already argued that '[w]e are not just anybody but *ourselves*.' For Barth, the penultimate nature of the particular bonds of nationhood and kinship notwithstanding, these bonds are nonetheless 'a living reality in which we all stand and which is certainly not ethically irrelevant.' We meet God 'in this reality and not another, that in this respect…God will find us where he has put us.'[35] This theme of (penultimate) historic and visible particularity is what Barth returns to in §49.3 of the *Dogmatics*, as the qualification to the uniformity of the common goal to which humanity is directed by God's ruling.

> [P]articular creatures and individuals and historical groupings and relationships are [not] prevented by Him from existing in their particularity and for particular ends. Nor does it mean that the particularity of their activity and effects, and the endless variety of happenings which go to make up world history as a whole, will later be ironed out and destroyed in favour of an all-comprehensive and unified plan. The Ruler of world history is also the Creator who has given this particularity to the various creatures and creaturely groupings. And in preserving them, He gives them room for their particular activity…He can direct all creatures to the one goal, and subordinate all other goals to this one. He has a unified plan which is in the process of execution, and there is no creature which this plan does not embrace…*But in its own place and in its own way.* [*CD* III/3, 167–168][36]

---

35 Barth, *Ethics*, 193.

36 My emphasis.

Taken together, these three general points regarding the divine ruling—the sole sovereign rule of God; the rule of God as the *ordering* of world-occurrence; and the qualified freedom of particularity in which creaturely activity can occur within the limits of God's ordering—have implications that are directly relevant to the place of Israel in the sphere of providence.

First, the reality of the foundation of Israel cannot be seen merely as the confluence of disparate historical factors (for example Zionism, the Balfour Declaration and the British mandate, the Holocaust), or even as the activity of God, inasmuch as that divine activity is held captive to or domesticated by human reason. Rather, Israel's national historic reality can be understood only by recourse to the sovereign movement of God in history that is in the direction of God's intention and goal for His creation. Second, the historical, political, religious and economic activities by which the State of Israel was brought into being are not denied a valid role in the process, but are seen as being free actions that, notwithstanding the dignity of their autonomous freedom, are nonetheless circumscribed by the limits of divine permission. Third, the historico-political actualization of the State of Israel in 1948 is indeed to be recognized as the emergence of the State of *Israel*, in all its Jewish particularity. If not of ultimate significance, Barth does ascribe penultimate and, as we shall see, theological significance to the fact that the nation founded in 1948 was in fact *Israel* and not any other nation.

Up until now, Barth has been discussing the divine governance of the world in somewhat formal terms that could (he is concerned) take on the appearance simply of an idea, or the 'philosophical development of a concept.' This he is anxious to avoid, for the Subject of the divine rule is not a 'supreme being furnished with supreme power in relation to all other beings' [*CD* III/3, 176]. The very notion of a supreme being is not, Barth insists, a legitimate part of Christian doctrine, inasmuch as it lacks content. On the contrary, the only genuine Subject of the divine rule, and the only solid foundation upon which the formal aspects of God's governance with which Barth has already dealt, is the 'actualised "I am"', namely, the King of Israel [*CD* III/3, 176–177]. Not only does Barth stress in this regard the unity of the covenant to which both Testaments bear witness, but he is equally keen to emphasize that the movement of God's governance is from the particular to the general, from Israel first and then to the world.

> The King of Israel is the One who according to the witness of the Old and New Testaments spoke the 'I am', and in speaking it actualised [*sic*] it for seeing eyes and hearing ears by acts of power within the created cosmos and human history…For the Subject who [is]… the King of Israel, is the God who rules the world…[This] King of Israel is the Lord who made a covenant with the twelve tribes of Israel, thus making them one people and His own people…In this event He is the One who initiates the history of this people, and in all that follows He is the One who directs and fulfils it…And in the New Testament form of the spoken and actualised [*sic*] 'I am', the King of Israel is the same Lord of the same covenant…[But this] New Testament community…is the community not of the Jews only but also of the Gentiles…a community which is destined to be a shining light to the whole cosmos, knowing what the world does not know, and looking forward to the culminating revelation of the King and therefore to the end of all His ways. [*CD* III/3, 177–181]

Significantly, Barth underlines the concrete particularity of God's governance by explicitly referring to places and times where the actualization of God's rule is most clearly seen. We have to think, he says, 'of definite periods in human history…And we have to think of definite places—the land of Canaan, Egypt, the wilderness of Sinai, Canaan again, the land on the two sides of the Jordan, Jerusalem, Samaria, the towns and villages of Judea and Galilee, the various places in Syria, Asia Minor and Greece, and finally Rome' [*CD* III/3, 177]. If, therefore, Barth's association with people like Buber, Schoeps and Cohn confronted him with a human rather than abstract embodiment of post-biblical Jews and Judaism, he was equally certain that the actualization of God's fatherly rule over biblical Israel (and therefore the world) was real and historically specific in time and place. What Barth says of Jesus' passion in his 1935 lectures on the Apostles' Creed is just as applicable here: revelation

> is not a timeless essence of all or of some times. It is not to be discovered by laboriously extracting such a thing as a timeless spirit or a timeless substance out of all times…It is essentially concrete and therefore temporal…Revelation is a *hic et nunc*, once and for all and unique, or it is not the revelation to which Holy Scripture bears witness.[37]

Notwithstanding the determination with which Barth insisted on the unity of the covenantal community of Israel and Church, and that this community bears witness in its history to the kingly rule of God over the entirety of creation, it has to be said that in this brief portion of §49.3 there are some regrettable sentences. In response to God's faithfulness, Israel is constantly disobedient, unfaithful, ungrateful and thus delivered up to 'the legitimate wrath of its King' [*CD* III/3, 179]. Moreover, the history of the covenant in the Old Testament is hidden in obscurity, the witness being primarily one of expectation. In the New Testament, however, the witness to the history of the covenant takes the form of fulfillment, of 'an all-powerful act which has come to pass' [*CD* III/3, 181].

Against this, however, we see nothing that could readily be taken for traditional Christian supersessionism. Soulen notes that the traditional paradigm of economic supersessionism seeks to render the existence of Jews a matter of indifference, not only to Christian theology, but indeed and primarily to God. '[The] ultimate obsolescence of carnal Israel is an essential feature of God's one overarching economy of redemption for the world.'[38] This is not what we see in Barth. That Jesus, 'the one true Israelite', is rejected by Israel does not alter the fact that Israel itself *and as such* is also justified by Jesus as 'His people'. The fidelity of God to His covenant and *therefore to the people of the covenant* is upheld, by grace, in spite of the infidelity of the people.

In this light, it is important to note that when Barth speaks of the New Testament community as 'the new Israel', his meaning is very different to 'the new Israel' of

---

37 K. Barth, *Credo*, (London: Hodder & Stoughton, 1936), 80. *Cf.* Rudolf Bultmann, for whom revelation is always in the present, and so it is impossible to perceive any divine significance in the historical person of Jesus or the historical actuality of Israel. See H.P. Owen, 'Revelation', in C.W. Kegley (ed.), *The Theology of Rudolf Bultmann*, (London: SCM Press, 1966), 44.

38 Soulen, *The God of Israel*, 4, 29.

Christian replacement theology. There is no hint that Jews have to repudiate their birth or circumcision to be or remain part of the covenantal people, even if their justification is not on the basis of these things but rather on God's grace (which is in any case what was true for Israel throughout the Old Testament[39]). On the contrary, the justification that has been won by the King of Israel has been won *for* them, *on their behalf*, and *then also* for the world. In other words, if the King of Israel's people now also includes non-Jews, Barth nevertheless affirms that it still includes Jews as Jews [*CD* III/3, 181]. In this way, argues Barth, Israel surely serves as 'a light to the nations' (Is. 42:6; 49:6,8). So, while in the Old Testament 'the King of Israel is [already] secretly the king of all the nations', in the New Testament 'His coming on behalf of His own people means that He is active and manifest as the Lord of a community of Jews and Gentiles...' [*CD* III/3, 183]. To state it otherwise, 'the Gentiles who have come into the community have no glory of their own...but are only engrafted branches which are borne by the root Israel (*not the reverse*)' [*CD* III/3, 184].[40]

That Israel has this global mission of being a light to the nations implies, then, an unbreakable solidarity between Israel and the Church. '[If] the King of Israel is the Lord of the world, He is also our Lord...[and so we see] in the election and calling of Israel our own election and calling...; in the unfaithfulness of Israel our own unfaithfulness...; in the faithfulness of God His unmerited faithfulness to us' [*CD* III/3, 194]. But in saying this, is Barth falling into the trap of abstracting the people of Israel away from their historical particularity? Seemingly not, for

> on the one hand, we have the election and calling of the people (the twelve tribes, and their individual families, and the members of these families in all their generations, but all of them bound together like a single man). On the other hand, we have the one Holy Spirit of the one Lord as the bond of peace which embraces the whole community, so that they are not like many men, but only one.

And who in fact is this community?

> The people of Israel with whom the Yahweh of the Old Testament entered into covenant, and the community of the New Testament which has Jesus Christ as its Head...are no chance conglomerations of individuals, but whole, and indeed *in the strict sense a single whole*, with a common guilt in virtue of their solidarity in obligation and responsibility, but also with a common justification and sanctification. [*CD* III/3, 190][41]

Michael Wyschogrod says the same thing from the Jewish side:

---

39 As Fackenheim says, 'The Tenach [*sic*] constantly castigates the Jewish people for their unworthiness...They were not chosen because of their size or power but because God loved them and wished to keep His covenant with Abraham...This revolutionary incursion of the Divine into the world of man is not preceded by any indication of any special merit in either Abraham or his ancestors. The election of him and his seed, then, is radically unmerited; humanly speaking, it is arbitrary; religiously speaking, it is an act of pure, divine grace.' See E. Fackenheim, *What is Judaism?*, (New York: Collier Books, 1988), 115.

40 My emphasis.

41 My emphasis.

Can anything but joy fill the heart of Israel as it observes the mysterious way in which the God of Israel begins to be heard by the nations? Is it not the faith of Israel that, in the fullness of time, the God of the patriarchs will become the God of all people...?[42]

The upshot of all of this is simple. There is no other conclusion than that, in Barth's view, the historic 'flesh-and-blood' people of Israel, then *and now* ('in all their generations'[43]), together with the New Testament community of the Church are the united form, 'the single whole', of the community of the people of God. In Zwinglian language, the community of God is 'an open house' in which there have always been members both inside and outside 'the commonwealth of Israel [*extra Israelis rempublicam*].'[44] Markus Barth puts the matter slightly more simply but nonetheless confirms the same view:

> Jesus Christ did not come in order to divide and to destroy, but to reconcile and to unite. He died and was resurrected primarily for Jews, but also for Gentiles, so that both might be gathered into one flock...The people of God is greater than the church. The church, the synagogue, and the State of Israel, as well as secularized Jews, belong in this people and carry its name, because, since the calling of Abraham, even those who were not loved are sustained by God's mercy and patience.[45]

This, then, is the 'material content', the filling out, of the doctrine of divine *gubernatio* (ruling), within which the history of Israel occupies such an important place. Not only is the actualization of God's rule located at specific times and places within Israel's history, but it is also actualized within a specific community—the 'flesh-and-blood' people of Israel, and then and thereby and in solidarity, the New Testament inclusion of Gentiles. In these places, at these times, and through this one community, the world-governance of God is actualized, so that the Subject of the divine ruling is indeed the King of Israel who as such is also the King of the world [*CD* III/3, 185].

The History of Israel as a Witness to the Rule of God

We have seen that Barth regards the sole sovereign rule of God over world-occurrence as being the general form of the specific history of the covenant between God and Israel. That is to say, that the specific history of God and the covenantal community of Israel and Church instructs us that indeed God is also Lord over world history as such. Thus, the divine rule of God is revealed through the history of the covenant, but is also present 'in a hidden form...in world-occurrence generally' [*CD* III/3, 196].

---

42 Wyschogrod, 'Israel, the Church, and Election', 82.

43 Joseph Mangina notes that the term 'Israel' includes 'not just biblical 'Israelites', but Jews from the fall of Jerusalem to Hitler's Germany...' See Mangina, 75.

44 *Die Bekenntnisschriften der reformierten Kirche*, ed. E. Müller, (Leipzig, 1903; repr. Zurich, 1987), 198, 42. Cited in K. Barth, *The Theology of the Reformed Confessions*, (Louisville: Westminster John Knox Press, 2002), 93.

45 M. Barth, *The People of God*, 71.

Importantly, though, Barth does not accept that the divine ruling is revealed for what it is through the day-to-day movement of history itself. At this point, we begin to encounter the answer to our earlier question of whether the establishment of Israel is a natural theological datum. 'In world-occurrence,' says Barth, '[God] can be revealed to us only in the light of the particular occurrence' [*CD* III/3, 197]. Of course, Barth is also keen to affirm that, in spite of the hidden-ness of God's rule in the sphere of world history, we would be wrong to believe that history as such is 'a raging sea of events which has neither form nor direction' [*CD* III/3, 196]. On the contrary, there is a definite and certain direction of world history, of which God is both the Subject and the *telos*; but that this is the case is only demonstrated through the specificity of the history of the covenant.

> The history of the covenant and salvation in which the King of Israel rules, in which His plan and will and acts take place and are revealed, does not cease to be a particular history...It is from *this history and this history alone* that we learn that world-occurrence generally stands under the same lordship and has the same relationship, because the King of Israel is its King too. If we will accept it from this source, we will progressively confirm that it is actually so. On *this basis* we can count upon the fact that all occurrence really has form and character, that there is unity and purpose in all things...From the very outset, then, we can acknowledge only Him as the Lord of all occurrence, as the One who is decisively at work behind and within its relationships and movements, behind and with the sequence of its events...[All this] can be true only as we have elsewhere, in His own direct revelation in that particular and sacred history, a knowledge of the King of Israel who creates this context. [*CD* III/3, 196–197][46]

There is, therefore, no accommodation given by Barth to natural theology, to the revelation of God through history as such. The fact that the entire history of the world and of the created cosmos is ruled by the fatherly Kingship of God is not revealed elsewhere than in its 'biblical form', which is sufficient and with which we should be content [*CD* III/3, 198].

On the other hand, Barth concedes that outside the Bible there are certain 'signs and witnesses' within world-occurrence that, while not being a second or alternative revelation, nonetheless 'have a special character and function...[and] stand in a special relationship to the history of the covenant and salvation, and therefore to that one revelation of the divine world-governance' [*CD* III/3, 199]. Barth identifies four such witnesses: the history of Scripture; the history of the Church; the history of the Jewish people; and the limitation of human life. They are, he says, a 'permanent riddle' in relation to the rest of history, and can only be explained from the perspective of the God who rules history. Consequently, these four witnesses are often overlooked or ignored by those who do not consider them from that perspective. 'Only those who have eyes to see will see them, only those who have ears to hear will hear them' [*CD* III/3, 200]. What function, then, do these signs of Bible, Church, Israel, and human mortality serve?

> In their creatureliness, and with their activity and its effects, they are no dearer to God than other creatures. But they do in fact stand nearer than all other creatures to this centre

---

46 My emphasis.

of all creaturely occurrence, this centre of the history of the covenant and salvation which is enacted at the heart of the whole…[and] they testify and confirm and demonstrate, from where and by whom that occurrence is ruled…As signs and witnesses they affirm that the One who rules is the Lord of the history and the covenant to which the Bible bears testimony—the King of Israel. [*CD* III/3, 199–200]

For our purposes, we shall not look at what Barth has to say about Scripture, the Church or the limitation of life in the context of their service as witnesses to the divine governance, other than to note that Barth regards their existence as no less of a riddle than that of the Jews. Barth has often been criticized for labelling the history of the Jewish people a riddle, as though that description was intrinsically derogatory. Mangina, for example, subtly alters Barth's terminology to make it appear that Barth regards non-Christian Jews as '*merely* a riddle'—a move that does indeed convey a certain contemptuousness. That, however, is not at all what Barth had in mind.[47] Not only does Barth *not* say that the Jews are 'merely' a riddle, it is also clear that when he uses the term 'riddle' he is in fact using it in precisely the same way as when he speaks of the Bible, the Church, and human mortality. The Jews, in other words, do not exist as a riddle by virtue of a supersessionist assumption that after Christ they no longer have any theological significance. Rather, the history of Jewish existence is a riddle insofar as it bears witness to the overriding truth of God's sovereign rule that is nonetheless hidden from direct human perception, and that it does so in a way that is also hidden behind a veil. The Bible, the Church and the limitation of human life are riddles in exactly the same way. That is, the four signs and witnesses to the hidden reality of the divine ruling are in their service as witnesses also hidden. It is only in this sense of a double veiling, which has nothing whatever to do with anti-Judaic theology, that Barth employs the term 'riddle'.

It is not of course enough, however, simply to show that Barth's description of Jewish existence as a riddle is not infused with a deep-seated anti-Judaism, as Mangina, Soulen and others would have it. We have still to consider what exactly Barth does wish to say about the history of the Jews.[48]

In the first instance, Barth wishes to emphasize the 'astonishing and provocative' nature of Jewish history. More than any of the other three signs and witnesses, this particular history, as an indication of the divine ruling, 'has a very special cogency' [*CD* III/3, 210], and it is the character of and reason for this cogency with which he is concerned.

Barth's starting-point is to claim that Jewish history only began in a real sense in the year 70 CE. That he does so is arguably one of the most problematic aspects of his argument, for it seems to presuppose that the entire history of Israel from Abraham to the destruction of the Second Temple is without significance. There is, naturally, a christological reason why Barth uses this historiographical framework, but the framework itself does not and should not sit comfortably, either with Jewish people themselves or with (as Barth calls them) 'historicists', that is, those who wish

---

47 Mangina, 185. My emphasis.

48 Barth's shorter version of the following section regarding the Jews as witnesses to God's providence was given as a radio address on 13 December 1949, and can be found as 'The Jewish Problem and the Christian Answer', in K. Barth, *Against the Stream*, 195–201.

to read Jewish history non-theologically. Indeed, the tendency to interpret Jewish history through a religious paradigm has traditionally been one of the primary ways in which Jews have had their historic concreteness abstracted into shadowy caricature. It is no surprise, then, that historians such as William Dever and the so-called Copenhagen School insist upon a non-religious interpretation of the history of the Jews.

Nonetheless, in spite of the historiographical interpretive flaw within Barth's reading of Jewish history, there are two points to stress. First, he does not in fact disregard the pre-Christian history of Israel as being ultimately insignificant. '[T]he content of the Old Testament is the particular…history of this people with God, or rather of God with this people' [*CD* III/3, 210]. That the Hebrew Bible records the covenantal history between Israel and God is in itself the guarantee of there being a deep meaning to that history. Second, that the 'real' history of Israel begins only in 70 CE means, for Barth, simply that from that time the Jews are fulfilling their Isaianic mission as a light to the nations. In other words, after 70 CE, there is 'no continuation of the history of the covenant as a history of God and this one people *to the exclusion of all others…*' [*CD* III/3, 211].[49] The question remains, though, how does Barth interpret the so-called 'real' history of post-Christian Israel?

> [I]n spite of the destruction and persecution and above all the assimilation and interconnexion [*sic*] and intermingling with other nations, the Jews are still there, and permanently there…not often loved or even assisted or protected from the outside by [other nations], but quite the reverse; usually despised for some obscure reason, and kept apart, and even persecuted and oppressed by every possible spiritual and physical weapon, and frequently exterminated in part; yet always and everywhere surviving…

In reflecting upon the Nazis' ultimate objectives, how right Barth is to say that

> Jews as Jews were not meant to have any continued existence. They were not meant to have any perceptible existence. But they always have had, and they still have today; and today genuinely so, and directly after what was apparently the worst disaster in all their history, completely eclipsing all previous disasters. [*CD* III/3, 212]

This, for Barth, is the 'simplest and most impressive factor' [*CD* III/3, 211] of Jewish history since 70 CE. Despite the myriad persecutions the Jews have had to endure, they nonetheless *do* still endure, having outlasted their neighbours and their enemies— Persians, Syrians, Babylonians, Assyrians, Romans—and having

---

49   My emphasis. While the emphasis and terminology that Barth employs here to speak of the beginning of 'real' Jewish history in the year 70 CE may be peculiarly his own, he is not of course the only one to insist that the destruction of the Second Temple signified a fundamental turning-point within Jewish history. The same thought recurs, quite naturally, within Jewish thought. Irving Greenberg, for example, argues that the crisis of the destruction—*Churban* —'was so deep that it could not be healed without a transformation of the relationship within the covenant.' One of the consequences of this new relationship was 'the end of prophecy; direct revelation is inappropriate in a world where God is *not* present.' See I. Greenberg, 'Voluntary Covenant', in S.L. Jacobs (ed.), *Contemporary Jewish Religious Responses to the Shoah*, Studies in the *Shoah*, vol.VI, (Lanham: University Press of America, 1993), 83.

even outlived Hitler's genocidal Third Reich, whose 'thousand years' would in fact have been dwarfed by Israel's longevity. That the Jewish people have survived such traumatic history is self-evidently astonishing. As Arthur Herzberg puts it, the Jews 'are a peculiar people [because] they have been expected to disappear, and yet they persist.'[50]

There is a significant parallel between Barth's assertion that Israel exists in spite of its history of suffering simply by virtue of God's providential care, and the view expressed by Eliezer Berkovits, one of the most influential of all Jewish theologians who have sought to find a place for faith after Auschwitz. Writing from the perspective of Orthodox Judaism, Berkovits has argued—coherently if not, for some, entirely convincingly—that the *Shoah* must not be seen as a *novum* of Jewish history but rather as one of many (albeit objectively the most horrendous in magnitude) other tragedies throughout Jewish history. From this position, Berkovits contends that Jews are forbidden to regard the death camps and crematoria of the Holocaust as though they were the only aspects of God's relationship with Israel. He has little time for those attempts to deal theologically with the Holocaust that 'deal with the Holocaust in isolation, as if there had been nothing else in Jewish history but this Holocaust.'[51] On the contrary,

[t]hat the Jewish people has withstood all the barbarous attacks upon it, that it has been able to maintain itself in the midst of deadly enemies, bespeaks the presence of another kind of power, invisibly playing its part in the history of men. The survival of the Jew, his capacity for revival after catastrophes such as had eliminated mighty nations and empires, indicate the mysterious intrusion of a spiritual dimension into the history of man [*sic*].[52]

Moreover,

For the Jew, for whom Jewish history neither begins with Auschwitz nor ends with it, Jewish survival through the ages and the ingathering of the exiles into the land of their fathers after the Holocaust proclaim God's holy presence at the very heart of his inscrutable hiddenness. We recognize in it the hand of divine providence because it was exactly what, after the Holocaust, the Jewish people needed in order to survive. Broken and shattered in spirit even more than in body, we could not have been able to continue on our Jewish way throughout history without some vindication of our faith that the 'Guardian of Israel neither slumbers nor sleeps.' The state of Israel came at a moment in history when nothing else could have saved Israel from extinction through hopelessness. It is our lifeline to the future…[In the rebirth of the State of Israel and its success] we have seen a smile on the face of God. It is enough.[53]

The similarity of Barth's position regarding the survival of the Jews and that proposed by Berkovits is instructive. However, it is of central importance to Barth's argument

---

50 A. Herzberg & A. Hirt-Manheimer, *Jews: The Essence and Character of a People*, (New York: HarperCollins, 1998), 1.

51 E. Berkovits, *Faith After the Holocaust*, (New York: KTAV, 1973), 88.

52 E. Berkovits, *With God in Hell: Judaism in the Ghettos and Death Camps*, (New York: Sanhedrin Press, 1979), 83.

53 Berkovits, *Faith*, 134, 152

that the astonishing mystery of Jewish survival is not to be understood on its own, but only in relation to who the Jews actually are.[54] How, then, does Barth answer this question?

He begins his discussion of Jewish identity by saying, with Augustine, that the Jews are the 'librarians of the Church'. What this means for him, though, is not that the Jews are relics of a bygone age. Nor does it mean that the Jews are those who have bequeathed to the Church the foundational Scriptures of Christianity that they themselves nonetheless did not obey. Rather, they exist as 'a constantly self-renewed actualization and demonstration of the man [*sic*] who in virtue of these books [of the Old Testament] was God's partner in the covenant...' In other words, the man before God, in both Testaments, is the Jewish man, so that 'if any of us wish to identify ourselves with this man before God in the biblical sense, we have to identify ourselves with this Jewish man' [*CD* III/3, 212–213]. This image of the Jews as an archetypal pattern to which non-Jews are directed for their self-definition is one to which Barth will return later in the section.

For now, however, he continues with an exploration of Jewish identity by considering those characteristics that are normatively used to define racial or ethnic groupings but, crucially, finding none of them useful in the Jewish context. The Jews are not, says Barth, a single race. In stark contrast to the history of racial science under the influence of people like J.K. Lavatar and Freidrich Jahn, and in even starker contrast to the extremes of Nazi racism, Barth insists that 'it is impossible to point to any specifically Jewish [physical] characteristics...[Moreover] the idea of a specifically Jewish blood is pure imagination' [*CD* III/3, 213]. Similarly, Barth rejects the idea that there is a particularly characteristic Jewish language, or culture, or history, or even religion [*CD* III/3, 213–214].[55] In all of this, Barth walks a fine line; on the one hand, he is keen to avoid perpetuating the racial myths of Jewish identity, but on the other hand runs the risk of denying reality to some of those things with which Jews have self-consciously identified.

If Barth's reluctance to regard as determinative those usual characteristics of peoplehood renders his discussion of Jewish identity somewhat ambiguous, that is because he has a wider vista in sight. In seeking to determine the nature of Jewish identity, his question does not revolve around the criteria of race, language, culture, religion or history. Rather, he asks 'what is admittedly a perverse question: Are the Jews really a people at all?', to which he immediately replies that they 'have to be understood as a people which is not a people.' This in turn leads to the inevitable

---

54 To try to define Jewishness is not so derogatory an exercise as it may at first appear. Herzberg and Hirt-Manheimer's book, *Jews*, is just one of numerous attempts, often by Jews, to answer this very question. See for example: M. Hyman, *Who is a Jew? Conversations, Not Conclusions*, (Woodsrock, VT: Jewish Lights Publishing, 1999); J. Steyn, *The Jew: Assumptions of Identity*, (London: Cassell, 1999).

55 As far as there being a single Jewish religion is concerned, Barth notes that synagogue-life is neither identical with nor representative of the Jewish people per se. Indeed, Jews can be pantheists, atheists, Christians or skeptics without ceasing to be Jews. Moreover, religion was not constitutive for the inauguration of the State of Israel. Similarly, there is not one Jewish history, but rather the many and varied histories of different groupings of Jews throughout the Diaspora, as well as the histories of various Jewish movements such as Zionism.

conclusion that with 'the history of the Jews we are dealing with a problem *sui generis*' [*CD* III/3, 215–216]. What does he mean by this? In what sense are the Jews 'a people which is not a people', and how is Barth able to avoid the obvious antisemitic overtones that such a description entails (if indeed he does so)?

In light of his doctrine of election in which he insists upon the solidarity with which both Jews and Christians exist 'under the bow of the one covenant', and in light also of his understanding of Israel's role within the divine ruling, it is hardly surprising that the premise upon which Barth constructs his concept of Jewish identity is that of election.[56] Irrespective of Israel's history of infidelity, God has nonetheless ratified the covenant which was made with them. 'Far from turning aside from His people...God not merely turned towards it but accepted solidarity with it' [*CD* III/3, 217]. It is by God's grace and faithfulness—not by race, language, culture or religion—that the Jews have continued to exist in the face of persecution and genocide. They cannot be 'overlooked, or banished, or destroyed—for the grace of God upholds [them]...[*CD* III/3, 220]. They are, in other words, 'a people...*only as* the people of God' [*CD* III/3, 218].[57]

> It is because the Jews are this people [the people of God] that it is true of them right up to our own day: 'He that toucheth you toucheth the apple of my eye. (Zech.2:8).' But no man can touch the apple of His eye. Therefore the Jews can be despised and hated and oppressed and persecuted and even assimilated, but they cannot really be touched; they cannot be exterminated; they cannot be destroyed. They are the only people that necessarily continues to exist, with the same certainty as that God is God, and that what He has willed and said and done according to the message of the Bible is not a whim or a jest, but eternally in earnest... [*CD* III/3, 218–219]

These are surely some of the most profoundly touching words that Barth ever wrote regarding the Jewish people. Not only does he highlight the failure, indeed the *inevitable* failure of all attempts throughout history to destroy the Jews, he also affirms that the Jews are not only elected by God but are indeed *loved* by Him.

It is of course also true that Jews, as those who belong to the eternally valid covenant, are unworthy of God's faithfulness. Their rejection of Jesus' messianic claims simply mirror their historical rejection of God as King in favour of a king like those of the other nations (1 Sam.8:5). It would be a mistake, however, to presuppose that, in pointing to Israel's disobedience, Barth betrays an underlying anti-Judaism. There is no shortage of Jewish literature that highlights precisely the same history of infidelity.[58] As Wyschogrod has put it, 'Barth is right...The history of Israel is a history of almost continuous rebellion.' Indeed, this insight is the one part of Barth's theology by which Wyschogrod has felt most deeply influenced.

> The discovery of Israel's sinfulness is one thing when it comes from a Christian theologian who believes that Israel has been superseded by the church and that Israel's sorrows are

---

56 See *CD* II/2; Lindsay, *Covenanted Solidarity*, ch.6; Busch, *Unter dem Bogen*.

57 My emphasis.

58 See for example: L. Kochan, *Beyond the Graven Image*, (London: Macmillan, 1997), 4ff and *passim*. Also, R. Joshua b. Levi, *Menahot* 53b, and *Peskita Rabbati* 160a, in C.G. Montefiore & H. Loewe (eds), *A Rabbinic Anthology*, (London: Macmillan, 1938), 94–95, 104.

the result of its obstinacy. It is something entirely different when it comes from a Christian theologian with roots in Judaism as deep as those of Barth.[59]

What is far more to the point than Barth's affirmation of the Jews' unfaithfulness, though, is his insistence that their service as 'bearers of light and salvation to the nations' is not in vain. More specifically, 'the Jews embody and reveal…what man is in the light of the divine election and calling, how he is an object of the free grace of God' [*CD* III/3, 219]. In the first instance, Barth acknowledges that there is a price to be paid for being the object of election and, therefore, for living solely by the grace of God, 'and [that] the Jews are paying the price' [*CD* III/3, 220]. All that counts for glory and value in the world is worthless; vindication within world history is an impossibility. The person who is elected by God

> is everywhere the minority. He is everywhere the guest and stranger. He is always the one who has no home, no city, no temple…Abraham was a stranger in the land of promise. Moses was a stranger to his own people. So were the prophets. The foxes have holes, and the birds of the air have nests, but the Son of Man hath not where to lay His head. The elect of God…will always and necessarily be strangers in the world, with no home of their own. In this sense, too, the Jews are the elect of God. [*CD* III/3, 220]

Importantly, though, Barth is not here reprising the age-old myth of the 'Wandering Jew'. On the contrary, he is quite deliberately placing the Jews in a direct line that leads from the Patriarchs and the prophets through to Jesus—a holy lineage indeed!

There remains, however, a more sinister aspect to the Jews' election insofar as they 'embody and reveal' the true nature of humanity, in particular humanity in its relation to God. It is in this context that Barth begins his assault upon antisemitism. Why is it, he asks, that Jews have traditionally been, not merely strangers, but in fact 'unloved and despised and hated'?

> How can we explain the strange disease from which every non-Jew seems to suffer in one form or another, the disease which can affect whole masses of people and break out so terribly, as it did in the Middle Ages and even more so in our own days…?What is it that we have against the Jews? We cannot explain it merely by the few not very pleasant traits which we customarily attribute to them. All peoples have their unpleasant characteristics. Why is it that, although we are indignant at the unpleasant characteristics of other peoples and yet pardon them, we can never pardon those of the Jews? It is pure illusion to suppose that on account of their characteristics the Jews are objectively worse, or harder to tolerate, than other peoples… [*CD* III/3, 220]

For Barth, antisemitism is meaningless, 'shameful and damnable' [*CD* III/3, 221].[60] Its *raison d'être* lies simply in the fact that in the Jewish people the rest of humanity sees its own reflection. Far from being worse (or better) than anyone else, Jews act as a mirror in which we see 'who and what we all are, and how bad we all are' [*CD*

---

59 Wyschogrod, 'A Jewish Perspective on Karl Barth', 159.

60 As a 'damnable' affliction, Barth returns to a theme from his 1938 Wipkingen lecture in which he stated publicly for the first time that antisemitism was a sin against the Holy Spirit. 'Die Kirche und die politische Frage von heute', 90.

III/3, 221]. The Jew may be and is the elect of God, but is also 'the man from whom the cloak has been torn off.'

> The Jew stands before us as that which radically we all are. In the Jew there is revealed the primal revolt, the unbelief, the disobedience, in which we are all engaged. In this sense the Jew is the most human of all men. And that is why he is not pleasing to us. That is why we want him away…It is the very fact that we know him only too well which makes his strangeness repulsive. That is why we are so critical of the Jews. That is why we make them out to be worse than they really are. That is why we invent the absurd notion of a Jewish race, which we invest with every conceivable unpleasant characteristic. That is why we ascribe to the Jews as such every possible crime. Our annoyance is not really with the Jew himself. It is with the Jew only because and to the extent that the Jew is a mirror in which we immediately recognize ourselves, in which all nations recognize themselves as they are before the judgment-seat of God. That is what we can never forgive the Jew. That is why we think we have to heap hatred and contempt upon the stranger. [*CD* III/3, 222]

Barth's intent is clearly to expose the sin of antisemitism for the absurd and ironic thing that it is. By our own antisemitic attitudes and actions, we simply confirm that we are and do the very things that we pretend are peculiarly Jewish. In seeking to smash the mirror in which we see our own unfaithful and disobedient reflection, we do 'the most perverse thing conceivable' and so prove that we are ourselves 'manifestly the enemies of God' [*CD* III/3, 222–223].[61]

Having said this, however, it remains the case that Barth's use of the mirror motif does not sit entirely comfortably in a post-Holocaust age. Barth is adamant that the obedience, faithfulness and status before God of non-Jews are no better than that of the Jews, thus the absurdity and hypocrisy of antisemitism. Nonetheless, 'the Jews' are depicted as symbols rather than as fellow-humans. They function as archetypal ciphers of disobedience instead of acting as individuals. So, no matter how much Barth's intent is to demonstrate that the non-Jewish world is at least as unfaithful and as undeserving of God's grace as the Jews, nonetheless it is the Jews who are burdened with being the true representation of that disobedience and infidelity. Barth may not have fallen into the trap of antisemitism or even anti-Judaism, but he has surely succumbed, probably unwittingly, to the threat of 'allosemitism' in which Jewish individuality gives way to an abstracted idea of 'the Jews' as 'a radically different other.'[62]

There is in Barth's view a second aspect to antisemitism, predicated not upon a recognition in Jews of our own sinfulness but rather upon a consuming jealousy. It is inconceivable to non-Jews, argues Barth, that the Jewish people still exist. After all the persecutions, pogroms and dispersions that the Jews have suffered they

---

61 In the reference to 'smashing the mirror', we can perhaps see an allusion to the deadly violence of *Kristallnacht*, 9–10 November 1938, during which thousands of German synagogues were burnt and the streets of Germany were carpeted with broken glass from Jewish homes and businesses.

62 The term 'allosemitism' (άλλος being the Greek word for 'other') originates from the work of Artur Sandauer and, more recently, Zygmunt Bauman. See A. Sandauer, *Collected Works*, vol.3, (Warsaw: Czytelnik), 1985, 449–452, cited in B. Cheyette & L. Marcus (eds), *Modernity, Culture and 'the Jew'*, (Cambridge: Polity Press, 1998), 9.

nonetheless still exist—even now having their own homeland—and thus 'def[ying] all outward and inward probability' [*CD* III/3, 223–224].

Even more irritating than the Jews' continued existence is the fact that they have survived even though stripped of all the securities of nationhood that are normatively regarded as essential to national survival. As Wyschogrod so eloquently puts it,

> The eros of the gentiles is threatened by the existence of Israel because this people, living in exile and lacking all outward manifestations of the state, the normal instrument of national existence, survives the mightiest nation states…while Israel, against all human calculation, endures.[63]

Neither language, culture, religion nor race have been uniform enough to provide a secure national identity for the Jewish people. And yet, says Barth, in spite of the Jews' 'relative and unrooted' existence throughout the centuries, Jews have survived *as* Jews, achieving 'the very thing which other peoples devote so much time and energy to achieving, [but who] at the last achieve only partially and imperfectly, i.e., the practical demonstration of genuine national identity and independence…[I]n the same unfavourable conditions [non-Jews] could never have achieved a similar persistence' [*CD* III/3, 224–225].

In other words, Barth believes that the survival of the Jewish people throughout history, even and especially through the Holocaust, provokes in non-Jews a jealous rage by proving the ultimate futility of all the things of which we boast and which we regard to be the assurances of our own survival. In this sense too, then, the Jews are a mirror, revealing that 'no one, neither people nor individual, really has a home in world history, that no one is finally secure, that we are all pushed about…' [*CD* III/3, 224–225]. The figure of Ahasuerus, the 'Wandering Jew', is therefore not so much a myth as a representative symbol of all humanity—we are all, Jew and non-Jew, 'eternal strangers' for whom home and security are in God and God alone.

But the Jews' survival against all possible odds presents one final challenge to the hubris of non-Jewish nations; that in order to have survived, the Jews must be the elect of God.

> Why is it that we are so unwilling…to be told that [the Jews are] the elect people? Why is it that we ransack Christianity for proofs that it is no longer so? But obviously, if it is so, if this people which is not a people is the people of God, if in all its world-historical weakness it is still the true people, a nation without equal, then what becomes of the rest of us? And what a frantic sin is all other nationalism! From the existence of this people we have to learn that the elect of God is not a German or a Swiss or a Frenchman, but this Jew. [*CD* III/3, 225]

Barth's unambiguous affirmation of the continuing validity of the Jews' divine election at once repudiates both the *völkisch* presumption of Aryan supremacy that permeated German popular ideology from Feuerbach and Wagner to Rosenberg and Hitler, and the equally untenable theory of supersessionism that, in Barth's view, can only be endorsed if one 'ransacks' Christianity.

---

63 Wyschogrod, 'Israel, the Church, and Election', 82.

More than that, however, Barth insists upon a Pauline reading of the trajectory of election (Rom.11: 17–24). That the existence and persistence of the Jewish people is and can be due only to the gracious favour and faithfulness of God, demonstrates that 'divine election is a particular election, that we ourselves have been completely overlooked…[It] is the election of another.' So, our own non-Jewish election 'can be only in and with this other…[I]n order to be elect ourselves, for good or evil *we must either be Jews or belong to this Jew*' [*CD* III/3, 225].[64] Or, as he put it in the radio address, 'we Christians have [the promise of God]…only as those chosen with them, as *guests in their house*…'[65] When, therefore, Michael Wyschogrod states that 'the nations who seek the God of Israel must meditate on the mystery of their non-election,' he is simply repeating, as a Jew, what Barth had already recognized as a Christian.[66] Despite, therefore, the christological centre with which Barth completes this section—that is, that the truly Elect Other in whom we find our own election is the Jew Jesus [*CD* III/3, 226]—the particularity of the Jews as the primary objects of divine love and care remains the testimony of God's providential faithfulness.

It is worth remembering that Barth was writing this well before people like Richard Rubenstein and Irving Greenberg began to question the appropriateness of affirming a post-*Shoah* covenantal relationship between Israel and God, and it would be unfair to criticize him by theological criteria that were not current until the 1960s. Thus, while we may still baulk at some of Barth's phraseology, he must nonetheless be credited with an unambiguous repudiation of secular and theological antisemitism, a thoroughgoing endorsement of the Jews' continuing status as God's chosen and beloved people, and a realization of the necessity of solidarity with them. A far cry, it would seem, from the 'reluctant admiration' of which Sonderegger accuses him!

Political Support for Israel as a Theological Necessity

Now that we have explored the way in which Barth treats the subject of Israel in the context of the doctrine of providence, we are able to consider more adequately the formulation of his political response to the Middle Eastern events of 1948. We have already seen in an earlier part of this chapter that Barth was embroiled in political controversies at this time. On the one hand he was urging a more clear-headed response from the West (including its Churches) to the spread of Communism, in particular decrying the naïve logic of those who were too easily equating Communism with National Socialism. Significantly, one of the key reasons he cited for insisting upon a qualitative difference between the two types of totalitarianism was precisely in their respective relationships to the Jews. The one thing that Communism was not doing, argued Barth, was the very thing that made Nazism so dangerous. Communism

---

64 My emphasis.

65 Barth, 'The Jewish Problem and the Christian Answer', 200. My emphasis.

66 Wyschogrod, 'Israel, the Church, and Election', 86.

has never made the slightest attempt to reinterpret or to falsify Christianity...It has never committed the basic crime of the Nazis, the removal and replacement of the real Christ by a national Jesus, and it has never committed the crime of anti-Semitism [*sic*].[67]

In matter of fact, Barth has here identified not two crimes of which Nazism was guilty, but one; the 'basic crime' of turning Jesus into an Aryan hero was ingredient to the sin of antisemitism. By adopting a Marcionite repudiation of Jesus' Jewishness— making him, that is, into a 'national Jesus'—, the *Deutsche Christen* were able to co-opt Jesus to their cause as the opponent of the Jews and, indeed, the 'first high-profile' antisemite.[68] In other words, a key reason why Barth did not believe that the West, or for that matter the Churches, were as threatened by Communism as they had been by Nazism was because of Communism's (relative) indifference to Christ and, therefore, to Israel.

On the other hand, inasmuch as he was urging a more restrained response to Eastern Europe, he was equally vocal in lending support to the embryonic State of Israel. At the level of international and interfaith engagement, one of Barth's first public instances of support for Israel was in the context of the World Council of Churches, the inaugural assembly of which (as I have mentioned above) was held just three months after the State of Israel came into existence. It was, he believed, a theological travesty that ecumenism could not bring itself to welcome Judaism as a conversation-partner. 'The modern ecumenical movement suffers more seriously from the absence of Israel than of Rome or Moscow' [*CD* IV/3.2, 878].

In the penultimate year of his life, Barth was compelled to write even more harshly—and sadly—on this issue, as the controversies over the political legitimacy of Israel threatened not simply the ecumenical movement but Christian unity itself. In August 1967, less than two months after the Six Day War had ended, Barth was invited to contribute to a collection of essays entitled *Jewish–Christian Solidarity in the Third Reich*. Unable to meet the invitation, he nonetheless supplied a brief note in which his political support for Israel was made clear. In it, he argued that the solidarity between Jews and Christians that had surfaced during the Nazi period, however imperfect it had been, must be re-constituted in an unconditional ' "Jewish–Christian Solidarity" today!' If such solidarity was not forthcoming when, once again, Israel was having to fight for its existence, the earlier solidarity from the time of the Third Reich would be relegated to little more than a meaningless artifact.

Barth's warning was not without good cause. As he says in the note with particular distaste, the Working Committee of the Prague Christian Peace Conference, which had met on 3 July 1967 in Sagorsk, had already pronounced *against* Israel's fight for existence (*seiner negativen Stellungnahme zum Daseinskampf des Staates Israel*), for reasons which (Barth says) lacked both theological and political sense. These 'otherwise respectable Christians' had, through their public statements, caused 'serious division' (*ernstlicher Entzweiung*) which, precisely in the contemporary context, must not 'under any pretext' be allowed to prevail. With tongue only slightly

---

67 K. Barth, 'The Church Between East and West', *Against the Stream*, 140.

68 D. Bergen, *Twisted Cross: The German Christian Movement in the Third Reich*, (Chapel Hill: University of North Carolina Press, 1996), 143, 156–157, 160, 195.

in cheek, Barth even asks 'by which evil spirits [*bösen Geistern*] were they [the Working Committee] led astray?'[69]

Katherine Sonderegger's response to this letter is to express happy incredulity. While she is clearly pleased to see Barth defending Israel, she finds it astounding that his defense of Israel can emerge from his 'deep anti-Judaism'. 'How, in short, can his [position] be reconciled with and derived from his dogmatic theology?'[70] Having studied Barth's understanding of Israel as a witness to God's providential care, it seems rather more accurate to suggest an argument that is in fact the very opposite of Sonderegger's. Far from being inconsistent with his theology, Barth's letter to Marquardt stands in the greatest harmony with his dogmatics. His theology of election and providence, especially as it relates to the continuation of Israel's history as a particular sign and witness to the overarching governance of God is exactly what enabled him to stand in such close solidarity to the Jewish people, both during the period of Nazi persecution and in their struggle against Arab aggression.

We have thus seen in this chapter how Barth's dogmatic theology formed the basis of his political support for Israel in its first tentative steps as an independent nation. In our final chapter, we will go deeper into the theological basis of this solidarity as we consider the last major doctrinal locus of the *Church Dogmatics*, the doctrine of reconciliation in *CD* IV.

---

69 Letter, Barth to F.-W. Marquardt, August 1967, in Marquardt, 'Christentum und Zionismus', *Evangelische Theologie*, 28, (1968), 654. Note that in this letter Barth repeats the confession he had made to Bethge in May 1967 (see Chapter One, pp.7–8), that he had neglected his responsibilities towards the persecuted Jews during the Nazi era. He was, he admits, more concerned with other aspects of the Church Struggle and as a result is 'implicated in the guilt' (*mitschuldig*) of the Church's failure to protect the Jews. I would simply refer the reader to my assessment of this confession as I have stated it in relation to his letter to Bethge, above.

70 Sonderegger, *That Jesus Christ Was Born a Jew*, 138.

Chapter Five

The Function of 'Israel' in the 'Doctrine of Reconciliation'

We come in this chapter to the crux of the issue with which we have been dealing to this point, the question whether or not Barth's theological understanding of Israel and the Jewish people was affected by his reflections on and experiences of the Holocaust and the re-emergence of Israel as an independent nation-state. More particularly, if his *Israellehre* was affected, how did this understanding manifest itself in arguably the most 'Christian' of all doctrines, the doctrine of reconciliation (*CD* IV).

Given that this particular doctrine is so tightly bound to the person of Jesus, we could be forgiven for expecting that here, if anywhere, we would find a sharp distinction within dogmatic theology between Christians and Jews. Hans Küng, who is in so many ways a keen admirer of Barth, has stated the problem in the following way. In Christian dogmatics, he says,

> the dominant feature is still a doctrine of the Trinity and a Christology which are remote from their Jewish roots, and built entirely on the Hellenistic councils of the early church. This is a dogmatics of the kind for which Karl Barth most recently once again laid the foundations in the Prolegomena to his *Church Dogmatics*, and which was then developed in what is beyond doubt a magnificent way in his Doctrine of the Reconciliation. But on the basis of a dogmatics which begins with the 'triune God' and 'God the Son', a dialogue with Jews is hardly possible.[1]

This is not to suggest, and Küng in fact does not suggest, that Barth was thereby unable to dialogue with Jewish people—rather, the point is that any such dialogue was and is not possible on the basis of his dogmatic theology, in particular his understanding of God's reconciling activity in the person of Jesus.

It is perhaps worth noting that Barth himself does not in any case regard dogmatic theology itself as a suitable site of dialogue. Dogmatic theology has a different purpose altogether. As he writes in the first part-volume of the *Church Dogmatics*, dogmatics 'is not a free science. It is bound to the sphere of the Church, where alone it is possible and meaningful' [*CD* I/1, xiii]. Similarly in *Dogmatics in Outline*, Barth stresses that

> the subject of dogmatics is the Christian Church. The subject of a science can only be one in which the object and sphere of activity in question are present and familiar. Therefore it is no limitation and no vilification of the concept of dogmatics as a science to say that

---

1   H. Küng, *Judaism: The Religious Situation of Our Time*, trans. J. Bowden, (London: SCM Press, 1992), 316.

the subject of this science is the Church. It is the place, the community, charged with the object and the activity with which dogmatics is concerned—namely, the proclamation of the Gospel...The man [sic] who seeks to occupy himself with dogmatics and deliberately puts himself outside the Church would have to reckon with the fact that for him the object of dogmatics would be alien...[2]

On the other hand, Küng clearly has a point. Barth's theology, not least of all his doctrine of reconciliation, *is* thoroughly trinitarian and christocentric. It would be unreasonable, if not offensive, for Christian theology to demand of Jews an acquiescence to the christological core of this doctrine, and so a certain amount of distance between the two must naturally appear. In this regard, Barth's dogmatic framework does, on the face of it, restrict genuine dialogue. Interestingly enough, the late Rabbi Joseph Soloveitchik used Barth's theological method to justify his own rejection of interfaith dialogue, on the basis that statements of faith arising from a particular tradition could not be understood by anyone who did not share the same tradition. Thus, in Soloveitchik's view, Barth was quite justified in shaping his dogmatic theology around an unapologetically Christian core—but equally, a Jewish theology should be unapologetically Jewish. If that hindered dialogue, then that was simply to be expected by virtue of the nature of the dogmatic discipline.[3] As I hope to show, in employing Barth's theology to discredit the legitimacy of interfaith dialogue, Soloveitchik fundamentally misunderstood Barth's intent.

Conversely, however, it must be admitted that the normative Reformed tradition, of which Barth was an inheritor and in which Christ's work of reconciliation has only limited efficacy, inevitably sunders any previously won 'Jewish–Christian solidarity'. In the words of Olevianus,

> The sacrifice of Christ, so perfect in itself, is both by the eternal counsel of God and by the high-priestly intercession of Christ himself, appointed only for those whom the Son of God has awakened to faith...Hence although Christ has suffered *sufficienter* for all, he has done so *efficaciter* only for the elect.[4]

Similarly, Cocceius denies that Christ was a mediator for all, and holds that 'the reconciliation has been effected [only] of those who were given to Christ'. Moreover, 'it cannot be said that those in whose flesh and blood Christ participates are his brethren and children.'[5] More recently, Colin Gunton has argued against Barth that, while Paul's letter to the Corinthian Christians may imply a universality of scope

---

2   K. Barth, *Dogmatics in Outline*, trans. G.T. Thomson, (London: SCM Press, 1949), 9–10.

3   J. Soloveitchik, 'Confrontation', *Tradition* vol.6, no.2, (Spring, 1964). See A. Brill, 'Confrontation in the World of 2004', Response to the Boston College Colloquium, Rabbi Joseph Soloveitchik on Interreligious Dialogue: Forty Years On.

4   G. Olevianus, *De Substantia Foederis Gratuiti inter Deum et electos itemque de mediis, quibus ea ipsa substantia nobis communicatur, libri duo*, (Geneva, 1585), 67–68. Cited in Heppe, 475.

5   J. Cocceius, *Summa Doctrinae de Foedere et Testamento Dei. 1648*, (Amsterdam, 1673), V, 109–110; Cocceius, *Summa Theologiae ex Scriptura repetita*, (Amsterdam, 1665), LXI, 20. Cited in Heppe, 475–476.

of reconciliation (2 Cor. 5:19), it does not claim a universal realization of Christ's reconciling work.[6]

In the context of the present study, though, it is vital to recognize that Barth departs from his Reformed tradition precisely on this question of the scope of Christ's reconciling work. Having taken his cue from Pierre Maury's discussion of election in 1936, Barth does not follow the typical Reformed paradigm. Rather, he insists, in the very structure of his *Church Dogmatics*, that covenantal election is the basis and presupposition of reconciliation. (§57.2). Jesus, says Barth, 'suffered also for [his enemies].' Yet, we are *all* God's enemies. Thus 'the contrast between the elect (us) and the damned (them) can continue to concern us only humourously.'[7] As we shall see, Barth's understanding of reconciliation is far more open than those that were proposed by many of his Reformed predecessors, and consequently holds much greater promise for Jewish–Christian harmony.

In the rest of this chapter, we will consider first the fundamental theological presupposition behind Barth's understanding of election which, as the first major section of *CD* IV/1, sets the scene and creates the possibility for Jewish–Christian dialogue. On this basis, we will then explore three of the most significant—and yet in some ways most problematic—sections of *CD* IV, to try and determine the extent to which the 'promise for Jewish–Christian harmony' mentioned above takes shape within 'the structural and material centre' of Barth's theology, the doctrine of reconciliation.[8]

Christological Election as the Presupposition of Dialogic Possibilities

In 1936, the French Reformed pastor Pierre Maury delivered a brilliant lecture at the 'Congrès internationale de théologie calviniste' in Geneva, in which he argued that outside Jesus Christ it is impossible to know anything of either the electing God or of His elect, and that both election and reprobation were properly understood only in the context of the cross.[9] The central thesis of Maury's paper was three-fold: first, that there is no election without rejection; second, that the decision of God to reject can be affirmed as a theological truth only on the basis of the cross; third, that if our election is in Christ (and if the first two assertions are correct), then our rejection has been taken by Christ upon himself. In other words, the only sense in which 'double

---

6   C. Gunton, *The Christian Faith: An Introduction to Christian Doctrine*, (Oxford: Blackwell, 2002), 163. *Cf.* '[A] grace which automatically would have to embrace each and every one would certainly not be free grace. It surely would not be God's grace. But would it be God's free grace if we could absolutely deny that it could do that? Has Christ been sacrificed only for our sins? Has He not, according to 1 John 2:2, been sacrificed for the whole world?' K. Barth, *God Here and Now*, trans. P. Van Buren, (London: Routledge & Kegan Paul, 1964), 34.

7   K. Barth, *The Heidelberg Catechism for Today*, trans. S.C. Guthrie, (London: The Epworth Press, 1964), 82.

8   Godsey, 9.

9   P. Maury, *Erwählung und Glaube*, Theologische Studien 8; (Zurich: EVZ, 1940).

predestination' is true is in the fact of its content—election and rejection—being fully realized in Christ.

Barth was immediately struck by the force of Maury's argument. As McCormack has rightly noted, Barth's own understanding of election was decisively and forever changed from this point on. Previously, Barth had concurred with his brother Peter's 'actualistic' position that 'God's electing and rejecting activity [is tied] exclusively to the event in which God reveals God's Self in and through the proclamation of the Church, that event in which it is decided…who will truly hear the Word of God and who will not.'[10] After hearing Maury's paper, though, Barth was compelled to modify his views. As he was to recall later, he was

> the one person who read the text of [Maury's] paper with the greatest attention…One can certainly say that it was he [Maury] who contributed decisively to giving my thoughts on this subject their fundamental direction.[11]

How, though, is this relevant to Barth's understanding of Israel? Simply, because his entire doctrine of reconciliation is predicated upon the indissolubility of the covenant between God and humankind which, on the basis of the christological core of election and rejection, remains as true of the covenant with Israel as it is of the covenant with the Church. In other words, the *berith* between God and Israel is an

> 'eternal covenant'…even where on the ground and in the sphere of the covenant there are serious, even the most serious crises: movement of disloyalty, disobedience and apostasy…We can hardly agree with W. Eichrodt that the covenant may be dissolved, that at its climax the judgment which breaks upon Israel means the 'setting aside' of the covenant…What is true at all events is that the Old Testament covenant is a covenant of grace. [*CD* IV/1, 23]

The reconciliation of God and humanity thus has its presupposition in the unshakeable and unalterable faithfulness of God to Israel which Barth, contrary to traditional assumptions, insists is based not on law but on grace. This idea is not new to the later volumes of the *Dogmatics*. As early as 1934, Barth had stated that

> anyone who in all seriousness wants to speak of law first, and only mention the gospel afterwards, on the basis of the law, cannot with the best will in the world be speaking of God's law and therefore cannot be speaking of his gospel either…It is not only hazardous and dangerous, but also perverse, to want to read the law of God out of some event different from *the* event in which the will of God is manifested to us in form and content as grace.[12]

---

10 McCormack, *Karl Barth's Critically Realistic Dialectical Theology*, 455. Peter Barth's paper, in which this 'actualistic' corrective to Calvin was set forth, was entitled 'Die biblische Grundlage der Praedestinationslehre bei Calvin'. For a detailed discussion of the congress, see *CD* II/2, 188–194.

11 K. Barth, Foreword to P. Maury, *Predestination and Other Papers*, trans. E. Hudson, (London: SCM Press, 1960), 15–16.

12 K. Barth, 'Evangelium und Gesetz', in *Theologische Existenz heute*, 32, (1935) 5, 11.

That grace precedes law means, for Barth, that divine judgment occurs within, not outside of, covenantal faithfulness. Even 'the story of the Fall and its consequences', and also

> the later resistance of Israel and the divine judgments which came upon it in consequence, [do] not take place outside but within a special relationship of the affirmation of man [*sic*] by God, of God's faithfulness to [humanity], which is self-evidently presupposed to be unshakable'. [*CD* IV/1, 27]

It is not, however, in and for itself that the covenant of Israel with God is unbreakable. Barth locates the continuing validity of Israel's 'special relationship' to be not inward but outward-looking, that is, as a witness and sign to all people. As Tom Torrance has said, 'the role for which Israel was elected was agonisingly difficult: to be the human bearer of divine revelation…[to be] the people where God's revelation of himself was earthed in the clay of humanity…'[13]

The meaning of God's covenant with Israel is thus that 'Israel had and has a mission', that through Israel 'the redemptive will of God is to be declared to all humanity' [*CD* IV/1, 28]. As Kendall Soulen has realized, God encounters humanity only in and through the covenant with Israel. Contrary to Friedrich Schleiermacher's 'Israel-forgetfulness', Barth 'identifies *and rejects* the…unstated premise according to which the center [*sic*] of the Hebrew Scriptures is indecisive for shaping conclusions about how [God]…engages creation.'[14] Michael Wyschogrod words it this way: that God 'remains inaccessible to all those who wish to reach Him and [yet who also wish] to circumvent this people.'

> Because [God] said: 'I will bless those who bless you, and curse him that curses you; in you shall all the families of the earth be blessed' (Gen.12:3), He has tied His saving and redemptive concern for the welfare of all men [*sic*] to His love for the people of Israel.[15]

Barth does not shy away from the consequences of this affirmation. Mother Judith's anguished cry in André Schwarz-Bart's *The Last of the Just*, 'When will God stop *miracling* this way?',[16] is the anguish of the elect who, precisely because they are the elect, are persecuted and misunderstood by the world. According to Wyschogrod, Israel is 'hated on all sides by those who contest its election…Instead of accepting Israel's election with humility, [the nations] rail against it, mocking the God of the Jews, gleefully pointing out [their] shortcomings…and crucifying it whenever an opportunity presents itself.'[17] Barth puts it this way:

> it is the covenant people which lives and cries and suffers here, which is hemmed in and oppressed and threatened, which is more than threatened, actually overthrown and given

---

13   T.F. Torrance, 'The divine vocation and destiny of Israel in world history', in Torrance, *The Witness of the Jews to God*, 88.

14   Soulen, *The God of Israel*, 83. My emphasis.

15   Wyschogrod, 'Israel, the Church, and Election', 80.

16   A. Schwarz-Bart, *The Last of the Just*, trans. S. Becker, (New York: MJF Books, 1960), 260.

17   Wyschogrod, 'Israel, the Church, and Election', 80, 81–82.

up to destruction...It is in this context that there arises the prophecy of the redemptive future of Israel in the last days. It presupposes the dark state of things at the present. It views it with pitiless clarity. And it does not overlay this view with the mere promise of better times to come. It does not offer by way of comfort the prospect of later historical developments. Its nerve and centre is the reference to an event which will terminate all history and all times, a history of the end. It is in this...that the Yes which Yahweh has spoken to His people in and with the conclusion of the covenant will be revealed and expressed as a Yes. [*CD* IV/1, 30–31]

At that time, says Barth,

It will be revealed to the nations that it is not in vain and not for its own sake that Israel was and is, that its divine election and calling and all the history which followed in its brighter or darker aspects was no mere episode but an epoch, was not accidental but necessary, that its purpose was not a particular one, but the universal purpose of its mission, that its existence was the existence of a light for all men [*sic*], a light which was once overlooked, but which then shone out unmistakably in the gross darkness which covered the earth...It will then be the case actually and visibly that 'salvation is of the Jews'. [*CD* IV/1, 31]

In other words, Barth insists that Israel's status in history is as a messenger of God's faithfulness to all nations. Israel's covenant with God looks beyond itself to the covenant of God with the whole world. Crucially, however, in and of itself the *berith* between Israel and God is nonetheless a covenant in which God has 'ultimately... nothing but forgiveness' for Israel [*CD* IV/1, 34].

It is, therefore, 'impossible' to regard the covenant of God and Israel as having been replaced. It is, on the contrary, 'imperishable'. Nowhere is 'there any question of its interruption or cessation. What happens to this covenant with the conclusion of a new and eternal covenant is...that far from being destroyed it is maintained and confirmed'. Even from within the New Testament's view, argues Barth, there is 'no question of a dissolution but rather of a revelation of the real purpose and nature of that first covenant' [*CD* IV/1, 32]. 'With an eloquence,' says Soulen, 'that has few parallels in Christian theology, Barth insists upon God's unbroken fidelity towards the Jews despite their disbelief in the gospel, a fidelity that will endure to the end of time.'[18]

In affirming the ongoing validity of Israel's covenant with God, Barth is reiterating the message of *CD* II/2. However, just as his affirmation of the continuing Jewish election was the necessary interpretive frame in which (and only in which) it was possible for him to employ Judas as a cipher of disobedience and rejection in §35.4, so too the affirmation of Israel here is the necessary context for interpreting his excursus on God's journey into the 'far country'—that is, the human realm of sin, death and decay, into which, of course, the Son of God came as (perishing) *Jewish* flesh.[19]

---

18 Soulen, The God of Israel, 93.

19 For more detail on the so-called 'Judas Passage', see Lindsay, *Covenanted Solidarity*, 289–298.

The Jews in the Far Country

The first major section of Barth's doctrine of reconciliation in which he discusses Israel is §59.1, the subject of which is the divine condescension (*exinanitio*) of the Son of God. We are faced, then, with the particular history of Jesus of Nazareth. More exactly, perhaps, we are faced with the 'aspect of the grace of God' according to which, while not ceasing to be God, God—in Jesus Christ—'goes into the far country, into the evil society of this being which is not God and [which is] against God' [*CD* IV/1, 158].

In earlier Reformed dogmatics, a distinction was made between Christ's *exinanitio* and the *humiliatio*, the former treating Jesus' 'birth and burdensome life', with the latter referring more specifically to Christ's death and subsequent descent into hell (*descensus ad infernos*).[20] In Heppe's volume, the *humiliatio* is accorded far weightier significance than Jesus' birth and life. For Barth, however, the emphasis is reversed. Barth's overarching theme is that, in the condescension of the Son of God, God became 'flesh'. Far more illustrative of Christ's humiliation than any descent into hell is that the Son of God assumed 'the concrete form of human nature and the being of man [*sic*] in his world under the sign and form of Adam—the being of man as corrupted and therefore destroyed, as unreconciled with God and therefore lost' [*CD* IV/1, 165]. But Barth goes further to argue that, within this context of the assumption of human nature, 'there is one thing we must emphasise especially...The Word did not simply become any "flesh"...It became *Jewish* flesh' [*CD* IV/1, 166].[21]

> The Church's whole doctrine of the incarnation and atonement becomes abstract and valueless and meaningless to the extent that [Jesus' Jewishness] comes to be regarded as something accidental and incidental. The New Testament witness to Jesus the Christ, the Son of God, stands on the soil of the Old Testament and cannot be separated from it. The pronouncements of the New Testament Christology may have been shaped by a very non-Jewish environment. But they relate always to a man who is seen to be not a man in general, a neutral man, but the conclusion and sum of the history of God with the people of Israel, the One who fulfils the covenant made by God with this people. [*CD* IV/1, 166]

For Barth, it is central to the Christian message that a Jew stands at the heart of the *kerygma*. Only as a *Jewish* man does Jesus also come into the world with a message *for* the world. It is only from within the sphere of Israel that Jesus can truly be what Israel's vocation was always to be, that is, a 'light to the nations' (Is.42:6). This is why Barth is so strongly critical of Marcion, the Socinians, Schleiermacher and Harnack, all of whom, in their own ways, tried to de-Judaize the humanity of Jesus and thus the essential Jewishness of the gospel, 'to the great detriment...of this very heart of the Christian message' [*CD* IV/1, 167].

This recognition of Jesus' Jewishness was not a novel element in Barth's postwar dogmatics. As early as 1924 he had been compelled to acknowledge, in a remarkable about-face from the presuppositions of his *Romans* period, the historicity

---

20 See Heppe, 488–494.
21 My emphasis.

of revelation. Insofar as we grapple with the actuality of the *Deus dixit*, we must also grapple with the scandalous particularity of the 'offensive '*there* in Palestine' and '*then* in the years AD 1–30' [*GD*, 59]. In Göttingen, this 'offensiveness' was not in the Jewish particularity of revelation's historicity, but in the fact that there was a historicity at all that, however qualified, had to adhere to revelation. Perhaps because of Barth's reluctance to grant history any significant place in theological construction, he did not at this time exploit Jesus' Jewish particularity.[22] Nonetheless, the recognition was there.

There remains, however, the question *why*, in his doctrine of reconciliation, Barth was so determined to insist on the Jewishness of Jesus. Given that, as we have seen, Barth begins this section by describing the humanity with which Jesus cloaked himself as perishing and sinful flesh, is Barth merely trying to employ Jewishness as the archetypal form of sinful humanity? In other words, did Jesus have to become Jewish flesh in order to be mantled with the most sinful flesh and so, in turn, to be able to atone for the sinfulness of *all*—even the worst!—flesh?

At times, this is precisely what Barth seems to be saying. The elect of God, 'the object of divine grace, is not in any way worthy of it.' Israel, as the son who is pledged to the obedience that arises from its election, most usually gives as its answer to that demand for obedience the response of disobedience. The history of Israel is 'a history of the most outrageous and fatal insubordination to Yahweh…' Moreover, it is the very fact that Israel is 'this disobedient son, this faithless people', that Jesus has to take Israel's place and no other [*CD* IV/1, 171]. Only by assuming Israel's sonship, and replacing Israel's disobedience with His own obedience, can Jesus act as reconciler, not only for Israel but indeed for the world at large.

> Without anything to excuse or cover it, without any appearance of the accidental or merely external, the being and nature of man [*sic*] are radically and fundamentally revealed in the human people of Israel…That is what anti-Semitism old and new has constantly thundered…The Son of God in His unity with the Israelite Jesus exists in direct and unlimited solidarity with the representatively and manifestly sinful humanity of Israel. [*CD* IV/1, 171–172]

From a Jewish perspective, Wyschogrod affirms Barth's point. 'Israel,' he says, 'tends to forget that its election is for service, that it is a sign of the infinite and unwarranted gift of God rather than any inherent superiority of the people.' More than that, Israel must 'come to terms with its failure, with the misuse to which it has put its election.'[23]

In fact, though, the necessary particularity of Israel is not, in Barth's view, a consequence of Israel's sinfulness being in any way worse than the disobedience of others. Jewish humanity is no more sinful than non-Jewish humanity, and so in becoming a Jewish man Jesus was not assuming an archetypal sinfulness. On the contrary, Barth insists that 'there is no [one] who…is not in the plight' of standing guiltily in contradiction of God [*CD* IV/1, 173]. What the antisemites fail to understand is that in the sinfulness of Israel we have 'a mirror held up to…all peoples'

---

22 See my *Covenanted Solidarity*, chs.4, 6.
23 Wyschogrod, 'Israel, the Church, and Election', 80.

[*CD* IV/1, 171–172]. In other words, the particularity of Israel's disobedience before God, and the fact that the Son of God assumed *Jewish* humanity, has nothing to do with degrees of guilt but everything to do with election. The peculiar fate of Israel is that 'the man [*sic*] elected by God not only suffers and experiences [his guilt]. He knows it. He knows that he must perish. He considers that he must die. The connexion [*sic*] between his guilt and the righteous judgment of God is constantly before him' [*CD* IV/1, 173].[24]

It must be said that Barth's language at this point is undeniably ill-conceived. To his credit, he consistently lays stress upon the continuing validity of Jewish election and, furthermore, on the fact that the content of this election is that Israel remains the people who are 'chosen and loved and blessed by God...' [*CD* IV/1, 174]. As he puts it later in this part-volume, no one can take the election away from Israel, neither can Israel itself 'in any crisis of its history...cease to be the people elected and called and commissioned by God' [*CD* IV/1, 689]. Also to his credit, Barth accurately voices the anguished cry of the Jews that has echoed throughout Israel's 'history of suffering', 'Where now is thy God?'

However, with the Holocaust only a few short years in the past, it defies comprehension why Barth here chooses to speak of 'the *scorching fire* of the love of God...' [*CD* IV/1, 174].[25] Irving Greenberg has commented famously that 'no statement, theological or otherwise, should be made that would not be credible in the presence of the burning children.'[26] Barth's regrettable reference to the 'scorching fire' of God's love falls far short of meeting this fundamental criterion. Even if it is charitably acknowledged that Greenberg did not posit this theological boundary until many years after Barth had written this section of his *Church Dogmatics*, Barth remains guilty of an awful insensitivity for which there is no excuse.

Having said this, however, the theological argument behind the terminology is in fact far more sympathetic to Israel than Barth's language suggests. I have stressed elsewhere that one of the most common mistakes made by Barth scholars is to short-circuit their reading of his theology; to assume, in other words, that what he posits in one section is not in fact balanced (or even overturned) by what he says elsewhere. *Latet periculum in generabilius*—danger lurks in generalities—was one of Barth's favourite sayings, and yet it is too often the case that Barth's interpreters have generalized one set of one-sided statements without seeing whether and where Barth poses the corrective. It is important that we do not fall into that trap here.

---

24 See also: 'In contrast to others it [Israel] is the people of the election, the calling, the covenant, and therefore of the gracious will and commandment of God revealed to it, the people confronted with the Law of God. There is no doubt that it knows the Law. It does not reject it at its root. It knows that its existence depends upon the covenant with God and therefore upon the Law of God. It continually returns to it. It is continually summoned to try to serve it...Not in spite of but because of this, it takes place in its history that Israel shows itself to be...what...all other peoples also are, but what is only revealed in Israel...' [*CD* IV/1, 586].

25 My emphasis.

26 I. Greenberg, 'Cloud of Smoke, Pillar of Fire: Judaism, Christianity, and Modernity after the Holocaust', in E. Fleischner (ed.), *Auschwitz: Beginning of a New Era?*, (New York: Ktav Publishing, 1977), 23.

Fortunately, there are abundant reasons, even within this problematic section, why we need not do so.

In the first instance, even though Israel is depicted as being the mirror of all peoples, Barth similarly depicts Jesus as the mirror of Israel. That is to say that if Israel stands knowingly under the wrath and judgment of God because it is the elect of God, the same is true of Jesus. As the one truly elect man [*CD* II/2, 51, 58–59], '*He* stands under the wrath and judgment of God, *He* is broken and destroyed on God. It cannot be otherwise...His history must be a history of suffering' [*CD* IV/1, 175]. There is, in other words, a solidarity of suffering that Jesus shares with the rest of Israel throughout their history of suffering 'right up to our own day'. Thus, says Barth, 'the Son of God...exists in solidarity with the humanity of Israel...He does not suffer any suffering, but their suffering' [*CD* IV/1, 175]. While he does not specifically say as much, there is really only one period of Jewish suffering within 'our own day' to which Barth could possibly be referring, that is, the *Shoah*. That he believes Jesus to have suffered in solidarity with other Jews in the midst of the Nazi death camps is a remarkable attestation of God's continuing care for Israel and, moreover, one that decrees precisely the same attitude of solidarity on the part of Christians.

In the second instance, while Barth does suggest that the suffering of Israel is, at least in part, due to the judgment of God, never does he say that this is true *only* of Israel, as if by its election Israel alone was destined to be uniquely punished. As has been noted elsewhere, whenever Barth refers to the 'lost and defecting Israel', he almost always uses the term in concert with the terms 'lost and defecting apostolate' and 'lost and defecting humanity', thus signaling unequivocally that the sins of Israel are neither more nor less than, but rather illustrative of, the sins of the entire world, *including the Church*.[27] More importantly, though, Barth insists that even 'in all His judgments' it is impossible that 'Yahweh would forsake His people Israel' [*CD* IV/1, 691]. Indeed, that Israel is not forsaken by God is proven, as we have seen above, by the Son of God sharing in solidarity in Jewish suffering.

The journey of the Son of God into the far country of sin and judgment is not, therefore, a journey undertaken purely on behalf of Israel, or purely on account of an especially sinful Israel. On the contrary, the continuing election of the Jews as those chosen, loved and forgiven by God determines Israel to be the necessary and appropriate place in which God, in Christ, condescended to come—certainly in solidarity with Israel, its life and its suffering, but on behalf of both Israel and the whole world.

The Royal Man

In the previous section concerning the Son of God's journey into the far country, we considered the essential Jewishness of Jesus in the context of the *exinanitio* of the Son. In *CD* IV/2, Barth opens up discussion of the other aspect which must always

---

27 D.E. Demson, *Hans Frei and Karl Barth: Different Ways of Reading Scripture*, (Grand Rapids: Eerdmans, 1997), viii. See also my *Covenanted Solidarity*, 281–298.

be kept in view, the *exaltatio* of Jesus Christ and, in him, of all humanity. This exalted Jesus, the Jesus of the resurrection, Barth calls 'the royal man'; but it is a royalty that, precisely because it belongs to the sphere of reconciliation, 'does not exclude, but includes, us…The royal man was there in such a way precisely because he was there for humankind.'[28] It is in this section, however, that we are faced with one of the most problematic parts of *CD* IV. If Jesus was and is there *pro nobis*, Barth is equally certain that Israel as a whole was *against* him. Consequently, Barth at times seems to revert to the age-old accusations of Christian history against the Jews. Are we to take Barth at face-value here? Or is there a wider theological agenda that keeps the possibility of dialogue and respect open? These are the questions that need to be asked in this section.

According to Barth, the means by which Jesus becomes the saviour of the world is the handing over of him to Pilate by Israel.

> The passion of the Son of Man is, of course, the work of the Gentiles, of Pilate and his race, but only secondarily and incidentally…It is not the case…that Israel and the Gentiles, Church and state, cooperated equally in accusing and condemning Jesus and destroying Him as a criminal. It is not for nothing that the one who initiates this action is the apostle Judas, and in his person the elect tribe of Judah to which Christ Himself also belonged, and in Judah (the Jews, as they are summarily described in John) the chosen and called people of Israel…It is Israel, represented by its spiritual and ecclesiastical and theological leaders, but also by its *vox populi* that refuses and rejects and condemns Jesus and finally delivers Him up as a blasphemer to the Gentiles… [*CD* IV/2, 260]

As we have seen elsewhere in Barth's use of language, there are occasions, and this is surely one of them, when he employs the most hostile terminology, seemingly without regard to its wider impact. In this particular instance, Barth appears to endorse, at least implicitly, the charge of deicide that, from the time of the Church Fathers until its repudiation in *Nostre Aetate* in 1965, transformed Jews 'into the scapegoat and whipping boy of Christendom.'[29] It is, for Barth, primarily and necessarily the case that responsibility for Jesus' death lies at the feet of Jesus' own race—and indeed, not only Israel's leadership with whom Jesus had had a running battle throughout his ministry, but the *vox populi*, the Jewish people as a whole.

It is, of course, impossible to accept such a premise these days. In spite of Barth's theological logic, his preparedness to keep the deicide charge on the table betrays a deep flaw in his theology. Despite his insistence that the Jews of Jesus' day 'were not wicked' but were acting out the drama necessary for the Gospel to be taken to the Gentiles; despite also the fact that the Jews who are culpable for Christ's death appear in Barth's account as little more than archaic caricatures with no resemblance to any actual Jews; and despite the fact that there is no suggestion that Barth regards modern-day, or in fact any post-biblical Jews, to be guilty of condemning Jesus to death, one cannot go along with him at this point.

---

28 E. Jüngel, *Karl Barth: A Theological Legacy*, trans. G.E. Paul, (Philadelphia: The Westminster Press, 1986), 128.

29 Lapide, *The Last Three Popes and the Jews*, 22.

On the other hand, the fundamentally sympathetic attitude of Barth to Jews, Judaism and the State of Israel that we have already encountered, as well as the danger of reading him undialectically, as if a one-sided argument was not balanced elsewhere, gives us reason to ask whether in fact this denunciation of the Jews is really Barth's last word on the subject. Without excusing his accusatory language, we do at least owe to Barth the credit of considering the wider argument that he is here trying to make.

Earlier in the section on The Royal Man, Barth draws the connection between the New and Old Testaments by noting that the faith of Jesus' disciples shown in the Gospel stories is faith 'in God as the faithful and merciful God of the covenant with Israel' [*CD* IV/2, 236]. It is not, however, until the end of this part-volume that he draws out the full implications of this connection. The merciful and faithful God of the covenant is, we read in §68.2, the same God who determined Israel to be called into existence 'in the great context of the act of liberation' [*CD* IV/2, 762]. Moreover, the fundamental presupposition of this liberating act, by which Israel was called to be, was God's free choice, based upon His love. Thus, God's love for Israel is not His *opus alienum*, but rather His *opus proprium*, even when shaded by wrath. That is to say, that 'God loves Israel...[is] an analysis of the actuality in which Israel lived and breathed' [*CD* IV/2, 763].

Importantly, though, Barth refuses to relegate this to history; Israel not only lived and breathed in the actuality of God's love, but *continues to do so*. The continuity between the Testaments is that God's love 'has not ceased to be the love which elects Israel.'

> If it is now said that God loved the world...this means positively that the purpose of the election of Israel...is now revealed as its determination to be God's witness to all nations. [But] it does *not* mean negatively...that God is no longer the God who elects Israel, or Israel His elect people...[The] election *is* primarily of Israel and not of other nations... [*CD* IV/2, 768][30]

In his last major statement on Israel in this part-volume, Barth concludes with these hopeful words: the New Testament authors 'look to the indestructibility of Israel's election and its status as the first-born of all nations: "Salvation is of the Jews"...' [*CD* IV/2, 771].

The Ministry of the Reconciled Community

At least since Cyprian articulated the soteriological formula *extra ecclesiam nulla salus* in 251 CE, it has been assumed within Christianity that the identity of the people of God is co-extensive with the Church alone. Only *intra muros ecclesiae* is it possible to enjoy covenantal relationship with God. As a consequence, it has been a fundamental presupposition of the Church—actually in clear contradiction of the *present tense* of Rom. 9:4—that all the benefits that were once the province of the Jews have been transferred to the Church.

---

30 My emphasis.

In recent years, a growing number of theologians have begun to challenge this restriction of the identity of the people of God to the Church. One of the greatest steps forward in acknowledging that there is a deposit of divine truth within non-Christian religions came from the Second Vatican Council of the Roman Catholic Church, in its *Nostre Aetate* declaration of 28 October 1965. Building upon this 'epoch-making shift in the relationship between the Catholic church and Judaism',[31] Hans Küng has argued that fellowship with God can be enjoyed within non-Christian religions, as well as by 'schismatics, heretics and...even...atheists if they are in good faith.'[32] Küng has no doubt gone further than many would wish or accept as theologically justifiable. It is true even Augustine accepted that the as-yet unconverted elect are part of the Church; thus 'the *externa societas sacramentorum*, which is *communio fidelium et sanctorum*, and finally also the *numerus praedestinatorum* are one and the same Church.'[33] But of course, in this scheme, the unconverted elect are simply Christians-in-waiting, and their communion with God becomes effective only at their conversion. Küng has clearly gone further than this.

However, it may come as a surprise to many that Barth, notwithstanding his deep commitment to the Church, was one of the first to argue along Küng's lines: that the possibility of fellowship with God should in fact be wider than the Church. In his so-called 'doctrine of lights', Karl Barth words it this way: that we may expect to hear 'true words even from what seem to be the darkest places.' There are 'signs and attestations of the lordship of...Jesus Christ, true words which we must receive as such...[to be found] with striking frequency...*extra muros ecclesiae*...' [*CD* IV/3.1, 119, 124–125]. Marquardt believes that these true words, these 'little lights' alongside the great light of Jesus Christ, are 'essentially...Judaism [and] Socialism...'[34] Thus for Barth, while the extent of the people of God 'is not co-extensive with the human race as such', the reconciling of the world with God 'has taken place *de jure* for the world'. Therefore, 'only God Himself knows the extent of this people', but it is without doubt a people whose membership far exceeds the boundaries of the Church [*CD* IV/2, 511].[35]

Embedded within this context are some of Barth's most profound words on the communal unity of Israel and the Church. In his discussion of the notes of the Church (as defined by the Niceano-Constantinopolitan Creed of 281 CE)—*una, sancta, catholica, apostolica*—Barth argues strongly that one of the few legitimate pluralities within the unity of the Church is the co-presence of Israel alongside the

---

31 H. Küng, 'My Encounters with Judaism', in Kuschel & Häring, 259.

32 H. Küng, cited in L. Russell, *Church in the Round: Feminist Interpretation of the Church*, (Louisville: John Knox/Westminster Press, 1993), 120. Note that one of the greatest steps forward in acknowledging that there is a deposit of divine truth within non-Christian religions came from the Second Vatican Council of the Roman Catholic Church, in its *Nostre Aetate* declaration of 28 October 1965.

33 See A. Von Harnack, *Outlines of the History of Dogma*, (New York, 1893), 362. Cited in L. Berkhof, *The History of Christian Doctrines*, (Grand Rapids: Baker Book House, 1996), 231.

34 F.-W. Marquardt, *Theologie und Sozialismus. Das Beispiel Karl Barths*, (Munich: Christian Kaiser Verlag, 1985), 254.

35 Pangritz regards Barth's 'doctrine of lights' as being in the closest proximity to Bonhoeffer's 'world come of age'. See Pangritz, 134.

Church. 'The people of Israel in its whole history *ante et post Christum* and the Christian Church...are two forms and aspects of the one inseparable community...' [*CD* IV/1, 669–670]. In this fundamental unity, says Barth, 'we are dealing with two forms, two aspects...of grace...*It is the bow of the one covenant which stretches over the whole*' [*CD* IV/1, 670].[36] Not only does Barth insist here upon the inseparability of Israel and the Church, he predicates this upon a radical rejection of the law–grace dichotomy so typical of post-Reformation Christianity. For Barth, law is not the mode of God's relating to Israel in the Old Testament, and grace His way of relating in the New Testament. Rather, grace is the presupposition of all covenantal relationships between God and humanity, in the Old Testament as much as in the New. With this recognition, Israel's religious life can no longer be discredited by recourse to the simplistic and pejorative assumption that it was essentially 'legalistic', in contrast to Christianity's grace. On the contrary, argues Barth, there exists between Israel and the Church a 'unity which does not have to be established but is already there ontologically' [*CD* IV/1, 671], on the basis of their common foundation in grace.

As we have seen Barth do before, though, even in this passage which is so clearly a summons to dialogue between Christianity and Judaism, he employs some deeply problematic sentences. The 'Old Testament man', for example, is 'the perishing form', the 'man who suffers the judgment of God.' In the New Testament, on the other hand, we encounter 'the faithful servant' [*CD* IV/1, 670]. While we cannot ignore or excuse such phraseology, it is equally misleading to assume that these sentences capture Barth's intent. They are undeniably careless, but they are not Barth's final word. In the same passage, and as its conclusion, Barth asks a series of clearly rhetorical questions. Of the Church, he asks

> does [it] no longer know the beginning of justification?...Does the Church not need to hold with Abraham to the promise as such?...Is not the faith of the Church based on simple hearing? [*CD* IV/1, 670].

The answers that Barth expects to this set of questions set the responses he assumes for his questions regarding Israel. 'Was the promise empty for Israel because it was not fulfilled?...Has Israel heard without in any sense believing? [*CD* IV/1, 670]. In the same way that Barth assumes his readers to reply that the Church *does* know the beginning of justification, so too he assumes that they will reply that Israel *does* know of its consummation. Similarly, in the same way that the faith of the Church *is* based on hearing, we are meant to understand that Israel too has heard and, to an extent, also believed.

This is not an easy section of the *Church Dogmatics* to interpret. At times, Barth refers to Israel in plainly derogatory terms. Nonetheless, the underlying logic of his argument points unmistakably to his conviction that the Church and Israel are much more than inter-religious dialogue partners. They are that—but they are because they share a deeper unity predicated upon grace, hearing, and believing.

It is only in this context of indissoluble solidarity that we can explore §72.4, which is the final section of the *Church Dogmatics* in which Barth discusses in any

---

36 My emphasis.

detail the relationship between Israel and the Church. In this section, 'The Ministry of the Community', Barth begins by noting that the existence of the community of Jesus Christ lies in it being 'actively for the world' [*CD* IV/3.2, 830]. Much like (and perhaps drawing on) Bonhoeffer's conviction that 'The Church is the church only when it exists for others',[37] Barth here argues that the Church's ministry is in service to the world. The world can rightfully expect that it will be served by the Church. More than this, the particular form of service appropriate to the Church is 'active subordination to God from whom it derives and *therefore to man* [*sic*] to whom it turns and whom it is to serve if it serves God' [*CD* IV/3.2, 833].[38] However, the world cannot rightfully expect to determine for the Church the nature of its service—that determination derives exclusively from God.

Barth describes the nature of this service of active subordination as witness, that is, as 'the proclamation, explication and application of the Gospel…' [*CD* IV/3.2, 843]. By proclamation, Barth means 'to cause to be heard in the world…the act of God in which it took place that He reconciled an opposing and gainsaying world to Himself…' [*CD* IV/3.2, 845]. By explication, he means that the Gospel—which, while not generally knowable is nonetheless rational—is rendered intelligible and unambiguous [*CD* IV/3.2, 846, 849]. And by application, he means that the Gospel is addressed not into a vacuum but rather is directed 'in every age and situation…to the whole human race' [*CD* IV/3.2, 850]. Within the life of the community, there are differing forms of this three-fold witness of proclamation, explication and application, including praise and worship, preaching, instruction and evangelization. It is in relation to the last of these that Barth returns to the question of Israel.

It is helpful at the outset to note that Barth distinguishes between evangelization of 'non-Christian Christendom'—that is, the evangelization of those within the *corpus christianum* who are 'Christian' by virtue of birth rather than conviction— and the work of missions. 'In mission,' says Barth, which is 'the sending out [of the Church] to the nations to attest the Gospel,' we find 'the very root of the existence and therefore of the whole ministry of the community' [*CD* IV/3.2, 874]. This affirmation of the role of missions may sound anachronistic in a post-modern world in which even some Christian theologians have begun to question the legitimacy with which the Church can justify its attempts to convert non-believers. Thus, for example, John Hick has argued in favour of religious pluralism, the idea that 'God' is 'a single reality that is accessed and partially revealed in all the major religions of the world.' Within this paradigm, Jesus becomes 'a person who *shows us* God rather than who *is* God.'[39] Thankfully, Barth manages to affirm the place of evangelism while at the same time avoiding the religio-cultural arrogance that lies behind the critiques of Hick and others. Strikingly, Barth deliberately repudiates the imperial-colonial view of missions. The only purpose of foreign missions is 'to make known the Gospel…'

---

37 Bonhoeffer, *LPP*, 382.

38 My emphasis.

39 I. Markham, 'Christianity and Other Religions', in Jones, 408–409. See also J. Hick, *God Has Many Names*, (Basingstoke: Macmillan, 1980); K. Ward, *A Vision to Pursue*, (London: SCM Press, 1991).

> Neither the aim to strengthen confessional positions, nor to extend European and American culture and civilisation, nor to propagate one of the modes of thought and life familiar and dear to the older Christian world by reason of its antiquity, can be the motivating force behind true Christian missions, and certainly not the desire to support colonial or general political interests and aspirations. [*CD* IV/3.2, 875]

As George Hunsinger puts it, 'evangelism can be motivated by better reasons than anxiety about the eternal destiny of others…' Barth, suggests Hunsinger,

> takes it for granted that faithful obedience to Christ's commandment, love's desire to share something exceedingly positive, and the uplifting prospect of imparting hope itself are sufficient reasons for the church to engage in evangelism.[40]

Having established the 'ground-rules' for proper missionary activity, Barth concludes the discussion by asking how the Church should encounter the Jews.

Barth begins his excursus by stating, what he takes for granted, that the Church owes its witness to Israel which is 'so promising and yet so alien, so near and yet so distant.' That Israel is a rightful addressee of this witness is, moreover, a theological given. In a sense, Israel is *the* rightful addressee, because the content of the Church's witness was from the very first actualized in and directed to Israel. This being so, the form of the Church's encounter with Jewish people takes on a 'highly singular' aspect [*CD* IV/3.2, 876]. Only in the most qualified sense can the Christian community seek to 'convert' Jews for, unlike all other nations and peoples, Israel has already heard 'the awakening call of God' [*CD* IV/3.2, 876]. Thus, says Barth,

> there can be no real question of 'mission' or of bringing the Gospel. It is thus unfortunate to speak of Jewish missions. The Jew who is conscious of his [*sic*] Judaism and takes it seriously can only think that he is misunderstood and insulted when he hears this term. And the community has to see that materially he is right. [*CD* IV/3.2, 877]

In spite of all those statements we have considered earlier, in which Barth betrays a somewhat condescending attitude toward Judaism, we see here an astonishingly more positive appraisal.

Barth provides two reasons for the illegitimacy of Jewish missions. In the first instance, Jews are not beholden to false gods. Earlier in his discussion of foreign missions, Barth speaks of all those among the nations 'who have fallen victim to…false beliefs in false gods' [*CD* IV/3.2, 874]. The clear implication is that this applies to all those outside of (and perhaps also some within) the *corpus christianum*. But now we find that there is one exception to this: Israel. To Jews, the Christian community can never presume to be proclaiming the true God in place of an idol. On the contrary, the God whom the Church must proclaim and from whom it has its own being 'was the God of Israel before the community itself ever came forth, and [in fact] to this day He can only be the God of Israel' [*CD* IV/3.2, 877].

With this perspective, Barth effectively rejects any and all supersessionisms. The 'Israel' of which he speaks here is emphatically *not* the 'new Israel' of the Church. It is, and by Barth's logic can only be, the Jewish people. Furthermore, Barth is saying

---

40 Hunsinger, *Disruptive Grace*, 12.*n16*.

much more than that God is the God of the Jews in the same way that He is God of all people. He is their God—but in a qualitatively different and uniquely special way. As he did in his (in)famous Advent sermon of 8 December 1933, Barth once more returns to the Johannine edict that 'Salvation is of the Jews'.

In November 1941, at the fourth Wipkingen Conference, a fierce controversy had erupted between two competing theological camps in Switzerland over precisely this issue. Both groups hoped to mobilize rescue efforts for Jews who were, at the time, beginning to be deported by the Nazis to the east. Such good intentions, though, were hampered by theological differences. The Zurichers, led by Emil Brunner, took the position that salvation *came* from the Jews, whereas the Basel camp, led by Barth, insisted that John 4:22 must be interpreted in the *present* tense. This was no mere side issue. On the contrary; Barth and his fellow Baslers were convinced that the Church's solidarity with the Jews, in Israel's time of greatest peril, required the firmest of foundations. Only the insistence that God's promises belong in the first instance to Israel could provide this foundation.[41]

It is this insistence to which Barth returns in §72.4, although the context here is not so much providing the basis for necessary humanitarian intervention, but for shielding Jews against the well-meaning but ultimately insulting attempts to convert them. That salvation *is* from the Jews means that their calling is 'irrevocable and unrevoked' [*CD* IV/3.2, 877].

> The Gentile Christian community of every age and land is a guest in the house of Israel. It assumes the election and calling of Israel. It lives in fellowship with the King of Israel. How, then, can we try to hold missions to Israel?

In a return to the argument he proposes in his earlier discussion of providence, Barth continues as follows:

> It is not the Swiss or the German or the Indian or the Japanese awakened to faith in Jesus Christ, but the Jew, *even the unbelieving Jew*, so miraculously preserved…through the many calamities of his history, who as such is the natural historical monument to the love and faithfulness of God, who as a living commentary on the Old Testament is the only convincing proof of God outside the Bible. What have we to teach him that he does not already know, that we have not rather to learn from him? [*CD* IV/3.2, 877]

Clearly, Barth regards the Church's debt to Israel not as something restricted to antiquity but rather as a continuing legacy. It is also important not to misunderstand his language. In referring to the Jews as the 'natural historical monument' to God's love and fidelity, Barth is not implying that they are merely 'fossilized' records of divine favour. Were this the case, he would hardly even have raised the possibility that Swiss, German or Japanese Christians might serve this function of memorialization. Instead, Barth's meaning is that Jews *in their Jewishness* are witnesses within world history to God's love—and, importantly, to Jews as the recipients of this love.

Katherine Sonderegger accepts that in this discussion Barth has transformed 'Christian anti-Judaism into a critique of political and racial anti-Semitism [*sic*].'

---

41 Busch, *Unter dem Bogen*, 375ff. See also my *Covenanted Solidarity*, 266, 279n.117.

Nonetheless, she believes that the honour Barth accords to Israel is ultimately a negative judgment. Judaism, according to Sonderegger, is refused endorsement as 'an independent religious system and institution...', and exists for Barth only as an ontological impossibility, as a 'tragic and perverse denial of [the] truth.'[42]

In other words, do we have in Barth's excursus on *Judenmission* a particular version of anti-Judaism, veiled in the guise of philo-Semitism? Sonderegger's criticism is penetrating enough that it must be taken seriously. There is no doubt that the second half of Barth's treatment of evangelistic missions to the Jews envisages a sadly desolate Judaism. In rejecting Jesus' claim to messiahship, the Synagogue 'became and was and still is the organisation of a group of men which hastens toward a future that is empty...[and] that is without consolation' [*CD* IV/3.2, 877]. Thus, argues Barth, the reason why evangelistic missions are of no value is because the message of the Gospel has already been proclaimed among Jews and repudiated by them.

> We certainly can and should hold talks with the Jews for the purpose of information. But how can the Gospel help as proclaimed from men to men when already it has been repudiated, not just accidentally or incidentally, but in principle, *a priori* and therefore with no prospect of revision from the human standpoint? [*CD* IV/3.2, 877–878]

It would be easy to conclude from this that Barth's rejection of Jewish missions is predicated upon an all-pervading pessimism of their usefulness. That is, that insofar as Jews have encountered the Gospel and have failed to respond to it, it has been shown that the task of evangelization is wasted on them. This, however, would be an altogether too-simplistic reading of Barth's theology. In a remarkable turnaround, Barth in fact affirms the necessity of Christian witness to the Jews—Israel is not, in other words, a lost cause—but in so doing turns his accusations against the Church itself.

According to Barth's exposition of Rom.11, which David Demson has argued is both coherent and faithful to Paul's intent[43], the only form of Christian witness appropriate to a Jewish audience is to

> make the Synagogue jealous...[The Church] must make dear and desirable and illuminating to it Him whom it has rejected...No particular function can be this call, but only the life of the community as a whole *authentically lived* before the Jews. [*CD* IV/3.2, 878][44]

But Barth goes on to say that precisely in this task the Church has failed. It has manifestly not made Jews jealous, because it has manifestly not lived authentically before them. Demson has suggested that Barth's approach scapegoats the Jews as paradigmatically disobedient; in a post-Holocaust world, though, Barth's otherwise profound exegesis should be recast so as to make the Church the paradigm of disobedience.[45] Demson, however, makes this claim only on the basis of Barth's *Kurze Erklärung des Römerbrief* and *CD* II/2. If, on the other hand, we consider

---

42 Sonderegger, *That Jesus Christ Was Born a Jew*, 142.
43 Demson, 'Israel as a Paradigm of Divine Judgment', 612.
44 My emphasis.
45 Demson, 'Israel as a Paradigm of Divine Judgment', 621.

Barth's excursus on *Judenmission* in §72.4, we find precisely the kind of accusation against the Church for which Demson calls. To this day, says Barth,

> Christianity has not succeeded in impressing itself upon Israel as the witness of its own most proper reality and truth…It has debated with [the Jew], tolerated him [*sic*], persecuted him, or abandoned him to persecution without protest. What is worse, it has made baptism an entrance card into the best European society. But for the most part it has not done for the Jews the only real thing which it can do, attesting the manifested King of Israel and Saviour of the world…in the form of the convincing witness of its own existence. [*CD* IV/3.2, 878]

When Demson thus argues that Christian enmity towards Jews is a 'sorrier history' than that of Israel's disobedience, and that 'our gentile rejection of this people is our paradigmatic rejection of Jesus Christ' himself, we can justifiably assert Barth's wholehearted agreement.[46] As Richard Harries has rightly noted, Barth's concern is 'not any attempt to convert individual Jews'; rather, 'the crucial issue is the credibility of the Christian Church…[in being] a convincing witness to Christ in its own witness. In this [according to Barth] it has lamentably failed.'[47]

Katherine Sonderegger's criticism, that in this excursus Barth fails to accord post-biblical Judaism—the 'Synagogue'—religious significance independent of the Church has not been annulled. It would seem that indeed, on this issue, she has a point. Thus, Barth's statement that 'the Church must live with the Synagogue…[as] the root from which it has sprung,' is not to be seen, according to Sonderegger, as a radical repudiation of Christianity's traditional triumphalism but rather as an indication that Israel finds its identity only in and with the Church.

In truth, however, the dependence is mutual. In Barth's view, Israel does indeed find its essential being in solidarity with the Christian community; but equally, the Christian community is nothing without Israel. Sonderegger is correct to say that for Barth the Synagogue has no independent existence. What she has ignored, however, is that for Barth the Church has no genuine independence as the people of God apart from the Synagogue.

---

46 Demson, 'Israel as a Paradigm of Divine Judgment', 621–622. We are reminded here of Barth's 1938 lecture 'Die Kirche und die politische Frage von heute', in which he says unambiguously that whoever is in principle an enemy of the Jews—even if in every other respect they are an 'angel of light'—is an enemy of Jesus Christ. See 'Die Kirche und die politische Frage von heute', in K. Barth, *Eine Schweizer Stimme*, 90.

47 Harries, 135.

Conclusion

John B. Cobb has suggested that interfaith dialogue can occur at five distinct levels.

> 1. There is Christian theological reflection that shows that in principle a dialogical relation to other religious communities is appropriate. 2. There is actual participation in such dialogue and promotion of it. 3. There is reflection about what happens in dialogue and how it can be improved. 4. There is the interpretation of other religious communities that encourages dialogue and shares its fruits. 5. There is clarification of the role and importance of dialogue in the total human situation.[1]

It may well be concluded that Barth was essentially uninterested in the third and fifth of these levels and, insofar as he attempted to engage in critical interpretation of other religions, notably Judaism, he was woefully simplistic and at times derogatory. However it is, I believe, equally accurate to suggest that Barth was both interested and involved in principled dialogue with Jewish contemporaries, and that he regarded Christian–Jewish conversation as fundamentally ingredient to the very being of the Church. As we have seen, he was deeply committed to the necessary Jewishness of Jesus, and to the covenantal bond of grace that binds both Israel and the Church to God and to each other. In some ways, in fact, Barth's description of the mutual interdependence of Israel and the Church suggests that he felt a closer theological connection to Judaism than to either Roman Catholicism or Eastern Orthodoxy. Thus in 1958–59 we see him saying that 'The modern ecumenical movement suffers more seriously from the absence of Israel than of Rome or Moscow' [*CD* IV/3.2, 878].

The question at the heart of this book, however, has been not so much whether or the extent to which Barth's dogmatic theology is useful for furthering interfaith and ecumenical dialogue per se. That is, no doubt, an issue of deep significance, not simply because many of the early critiques of the World Council of Churches were predicated upon the rather simplistic belief that the ecumenical movement was thoroughly 'Barthian', and thus entirely misplaced. I would hope, not without some justification, that further study of Barth's theology—perhaps especially in reference to his 'doctrine of lights'—would in fact uncover fruitful material for inter-confessional and interfaith cooperation. That is not, though, the question that motivates this study. Rather, the underlying question has been whether or the extent to which Barth's post-Holocaust theology, in particular his doctrine of reconciliation, displays a maturing of his understanding of Israel and the Jewish people.

In spite of his many detractors amongst both historians and theologians, it is a matter of historical record that Barth engaged both personally and theologically with Jews, as friends, colleagues and fellow-scholars. This is not to deny that, unlike Bultmann, Barth was never enthused by the study of Judaism as such. Nor is it to deny

---

1   J.B. Cobb, 'Inter-religious Dialogue, World Ethics and the Problem of the *Humanum*', in Kuschel & Häring, 283.

that, in many of his excurses, he paints an overly-simplistic caricature of post-biblical Judaism. It is, however, to argue that Barth was not as blind to contemporary Jewish scholarship, or as alienated from individual Jews, as has often been portrayed.

Barth was also a vocal opponent of Hitler's antisemitic genocidal program, and he articulated his protests within both the ecclesiastical and the political arenas. As a leader of the Confessing Church and principal author of the Barmen Declaration, Barth resisted the nazification—and with it, the inevitable Aryanization—of the German Evangelical Church. As a political activist, Barth provided support for Heinrich Grüber and Gertrud Staewen, he mobilized the Swiss government in response to the Hungarian crisis of 1944, and even on occasion gave shelter to Jewish refugees. He was, in other words, keenly aware of the Jewish plight during the Nazi years, and spoke out in open protest against their persecution. But in his post-war theological reflections, did this awareness have any material impact upon his formulation of doctrine?

In considering Barth's extended excursus on the existence and nature of radical evil, I have argued that, although it was written after the *Shoah*, there is no material engagement with that particular cataclysm. It would be both uncharitable and inaccurate to suggest that this lacuna is due to an ambivalence about the Jewish catastrophe; as we have seen, Barth was aware of the Nazis' war against the Jews and deeply involved in protesting against it. Similarly, his failure to confront the impact of the Holocaust within his discussion of *das Nichtige* cannot be put down to an underlying antisemitism. Rather, the absence of the Holocaust as a dominant theme within Barth's doctrine of evil is more appropriately explained by his resistance to any form of natural theology.

Until the end of the First World War, Barth was open to the possibility that God's revelation could be mediated through historical events and movements, such as Religious Socialism and even the war itself. From the time of *Romans* I, however, Barth became convinced that there was a necessary qualitative difference between revelation and history. With the rise of Nazism and the correlative German Christian belief that Hitler embodied the new revelation of God, Barth's repudiation of natural theology became entrenched. In the context of the Nazi heresy, this uncompromising theological stance was sorely needed; indeed it could well be argued that without this bulwark the German Church too would have fallen victim to the homogenizing policy of *Gleichschaltung*. As necessary as this was during the Hitler years, however, it was precisely Barth's rejection of the legitimacy of natural theology that precluded him from perceiving in the Holocaust any theological significance.

Having made this claim, there is an immediate need to qualify it. We have seen that in later volumes of the *Dogmatics*, Barth does seem prepared to accord theological weight to some patterns within history. In his exploration of providence, for example, Barth highlights the history of the Jewish people—especially in the light of the 1948 proclamation of Israel's independence—as a 'sign and witness' of God's providential governance. Certainly, this aspect of history does not, in Barth's mind, have the status of revelation, and thus we cannot claim that Barth has repealed his prohibition of natural theology. Nonetheless, there is a clear recognition that, in the span of Israel's history, we can perceive a history that stands in a unique relationship to God. According to Barth, the history of the Jewish people demonstrates, like no other history can, that to be loved by God is to be hated by humanity. Paradoxically, however, this history also demonstrates—especially through the events of 1948— the remarkable providential care of God, that enables life and hope even through trauma, and compels us to realize that, if we wish to have a share in it, we must join in solidarity with the Jewish people, who were and are its first recipients.

This present study has also sought to demonstrate that in *CD* IV, Barth's formulation of the specifically Christian doctrine of reconciliation cannot be properly understood without explicit reference to the Jewish people. Whereas it could well be assumed that for a Christian theologian to speak of reconciliation would be to speak in rather exclusive terms of Jesus and the Church, Barth challenges such assumptions by critiquing the very basis of much Christian anti-Judaism. In the same way that Will Herberg did from the Jewish side, we have seen that Barth begins his treatment of reconciliation with an insistence that grace suffuses the Hebrew as much as the Christian Scriptures.[2] On this understanding, Barth argues for an ontological unity between Israel and the Church. Moreover, this unity is not merely a relic of the biblical age, but remains in force; the Jews, insists Barth, remain loved and elect by God right up to the present day, *irrespective* of their attitude to Jesus. It has to be acknowledged that Katherine Sonderegger's criticism, that Barth does not accord Judaism any lasting legitimacy as an independent religious system, retains a certain cogency. I have tried to show, however, that even at this late stage of the *Dogmatics* there remains an element of dialectic. In other words, the relationship between Judaism and Christianity is not as one-sided as Sonderegger suggests. If Judaism needs the witness of the Church, so too the Church needs the witness of the Synagogue as the indispensable root from which it has sprung and in which it must remain if it is to be complete.

To return to the basic question of the book, though, is it possible that Barth's fundamentally sympathetic understanding of Judaism can be traced to his reflections on and awareness of the Holocaust? This, it seems, is still an open question. There is no doubt that the suffering of the Jewish people during the Nazi years caused Barth significant anguish, and that he was keenly and prophetically aware of the failure of the Church to provide adequate protection or protest. If one reads Barth's wartime writings it is abundantly clear that as the Jews' situation became more dire, his pleas for assistance on their behalf, and his protests against the German regime, became increasingly urgent. It is perhaps not surprising, therefore, that Barth saw the miraculous hand of God behind the proclamation of the Israeli State in 1948. It would be a stretch to suggest that this represented for Barth a softening of his repudiation of natural theology. The fact that one could perceive the work of God in this event was not, for Barth, a function of the historical event itself but was rather purely attributable to God. Furthermore, if Barth had moderated his stance on natural theology in relation to the creation of Israel, why did he not incorporate the theological lessons of the Holocaust into his discussion of evil which, after all, occurs in a later section of the same volume as his discussion of providence?

Nonetheless, even if we grant that the theological status of the creation of Israel as a 'sign and witness' is not the same as according it a natural theological function,

---

2 See Harries, 176–177.

there is no doubt that Barth's late dogmatic theology attributes to Israel a far more prominent and positive role than we see in the (pre-Holocaust) first half of the *Church Dogmatics*. And indeed, perhaps this is just as well, for it enables us to suggest that the notable progress that Barth did make in his own appreciation of Israel as a necessary ingredient to Christian witness was based, not upon a sympathy born of the *Shoah*, but rather upon an ever-increasing affirmation of Judaism as such.

Bibliography

Primary Literature: Karl Barth

Unpublished works

Letter, C. von Kirschbaum to Paul Vogt, 12 November 1938, Karl Barth-Archiv.
'Einladung', December 1938, Karl Barth-Archiv.
Letter, C. von Kirschbaum to Paul Vogt, 27 January 1939, Karl Barth-Archiv.
Letter, C. von Kirschbaum to Pfr. Rhenus Gelpke, 7 June 1939, Karl Barth-Archiv.
Letter, K. Barth to E. Nobs, 25 June 1944, Karl Barth-Archiv.
Letter, K. Barth *et al* to the Swiss Federal Council, 4 July 1944, Karl Barth-Archiv.

Published works (sermons and letters)

'Der Christliche Glaube und die Geschichte', in *Schweizerischer Theologische Zeitschrift*, 29 (1912).
Predigten, 1914, ed. U. & J. Fähler, (Zürich: TVZ, 1974). *The Word of God and the Word of Man*, trans. D. Horton, (Gloucester, MA: Peter Smith, 1978).
Briefwechsel Karl Barth–Eduard Thurneysen, 1913–1921, (Zürich: Evangelischer Verlag, 1973).
'Nein! Antwort am Emil Brunner', in *Theologische Existenz heute*, 9, (1934).
'Evangelium und Gesetz', in *Theologische Existenz heute*, 32, (1935).
Karl Barth–Rudolf Bultmann Letters, 1922–1966, ed. B. Jaspert, trans. G.W. Bromiley, (Edinburgh: T & T Clark, 1982).
Karl Barth–K.H. Miskotte: Briefwechsel 1924–1968, ed. H. Stoevesandt, (Zürich: TVZ, 1991).
Letters 1961–1968, ed. J. Fangmeier & H. Stoevesandt, trans. G.W. Bromiley, (Edinburgh: T & T Clark, 1981).

Published works (books)

Der Römerbrief, erste Fassung, (G.A. Bäschlin, 1919; repr. Zürich: TVZ, 1985).
The Epistle to the Romans, trans. E.C. Hoskyns, (London: Oxford University Press, 1933; repr. 1968).
The Theology of the Reformed Confessions, trans D.J. & J.G. Guder, (Louisville: Westminster John Knox Press, 2002).
The Göttingen Dogmatics: Instruction in the Christian Religion, vol.1, trans. G.W. Bromiley, ed. H. Reiffen, (Grand Rapids: Eerdmans, 1991).
Die christliche Dogmatik im Entwurf: Die Lehre vom Worte Gottes. Prolegomena zur chistlichen Dogmatik, (Munich: Christian Kaiser Verlag, 1927; rev. edn Zürich: TVZ, 1982).

Ethics, trans. G.W. Bromiley, (Edinburgh: T & T Clark, 1981).

Theologische Existenz heute, (Munich: Christian Kaiser Verlag, 1933); ET *Theological Existence Today*, (London: Hodder & Stoughton, 1933).

Credo, (London: Hodder & Stoughton, 1936).

Eine Schweizer Stimme, 1938–1945, (Evangelischer Verlag, 1945; repr. Zürich: Theologische Verlag, 1985).

Dogmatics in Outline, trans. G.T. Thomson, (London: SCM Press, 1949).

The Heidelberg Catechism for Today, trans. S.C. Guthrie, (London: The Epworth Press, 1964).

Against the Stream: Shorter Post-War Writings, 1946–1952, trans. E.M. Delacour & S. Godman, (London: SCM Press, 1954).

Evangelical Theology: An Introduction, (London: Collins, 1965).

God Here and Now, trans. P. Van Buren, (London: Routledge & Kegan Paul, 1964).

Church Dogmatics, ed. & trans., G.W. Bromiley & T.F. Torrance, (Edinburgh: T & T Clark, 1936–1969).

Secondary Literature

Books

Balthasar, H.U. von. *Karl Barth: Darstellung und Deutung Seiner Theologie*, (Köln: Jakob Hegner, 1951); ET *The Theology of Karl Barth: Exposition and Interpretation*, trans. E.T. Oakes, S.J., (San Francisco: Ignatius Press, 1992).

Barth, M. *The People of God*, (Sheffield: JSOT Press, 1983).

Beintker, *Die Dialecktik in der 'dialektischen Theologie' Karl Barths*, (Munich: Christian Kaiser Verlag, 1987).

Berenbaum, M. & Peck, A.J. (eds). *The Holocaust and History: the known, the unknown, the disputed, and the re-examined*, (Bloomington: Indiana University Press, 2002).

Bergen, D. *Twisted Cross: The German Christian Movement in the Third Reich*, (Chapel Hill: University of North Carolina Press, 1996).

Berkhof, L. *The History of Christian Doctrines*, (Grand Rapids: Baker Book House, 1996).

Berkouwer, G.C. *The Triumph of Grace in the Theology of Karl Barth*, trans. H.R. Boer, (Grand Rapids: Eerdmans, 1956).

Berkovits, E. *Faith After the Holocaust*, (New York: KTAV, 1973).

Berkovits, E. *With God in Hell: Judaism in the Ghettos and Death Camps*, (New York: Sanhedrin Press, 1979).

Bonhoeffer, D. *Gesammelte Schriften*, 6 vols., ed. E. Bethge, (Munich: Christian Kaiser Verlag, 1954–78).

Bonhoeffer, D. *Letters and Papers from Prison*, ed. E. Bethge, (London: SCM Press, 1971).

Bowden, J. *Karl Barth*, (London: SCM Press, 1971).

Braham, R.L. *The Politics of Genocide: The Holocaust in Hungary*, 2 vols, (New York: Columbia University Press, 1981).

Braham, R.L. (ed.). *Perspectives on the Holocaust*, (Boston: Kluwer-Nijhoff Publishing, 1983).

Brooks, R. (ed.). *Unanswered Questions: Theological Views of Jewish–Catholic Relations*, (Notre Dame: University of Notre Dame Press, 1988).

Brown, B. *Boundaries of our Habitations*, (New York: SUNY Press, 1994).

Browning, C.R. *Ordinary Men: Reserve Police Battalion 101 and the 'Final Solution' in Poland*, (New York: Aaron Asher Books, 1992).

Brunner, E. *Natur und Gnade*, (Tübingen: Mohr, 1934).

Buber, M. *I and Thou*, trans R.G. Smith, (New York: Charles Scribner's Sons, 1954).

Busch, E. *Karl Barth: His Life from Letters and Autobiographical Texts*, trans. J. Bowden, (Grand Rapids: Eerdmans, 1994).

Busch, E. *Unter dem Bogen des einen Bundes: Karl Barth und die Juden 1933–1945*, (Neukirchen-Vluyn: Neukirchener Verlag, 1996).

Casalis, G. *A Portrait of Karl Barth*, (New York: Doubleday & Co., 1964).

Cheyette, B. & Marcus, L. (eds). *Modernity, Culture and 'the Jew'*, (Cambridge: Polity Press, 1998).

Cohen, A. *The Tremendum*, (New York: Crossroad, 1981).

Croner, H. (ed.). *More Stepping Stones to Jewish–Christian Relations*, (New York: Stimulus Books/Paulist Press, 1985).

Cunliffe-Jones, H. (ed.). *A History of Christian Doctrine*, (Philadelphia: Fortress Press, 1980).

Demson, D.E. *Hans Frei and Karl Barth: Different Ways of Reading Scripture*, (Grand Rapids: Eerdmans, 1997).

Eckardt, A.L & Eckardt, A.R. *Long Night's Journey Into Day: A Revised Retrospective on the Holocaust*, (Detroit: Wayne State University Press, 1988).

Fackenheim, E. *God's Presence in History*, (New York, 1970).

Fackenheim, E. *What is Judaism?*, (New York: Collier Books, 1988).

Fackenheim, E. *To Mend the World: Foundations of Post-Holocaust Jewish Thought*, (New York: Schocken Books, 1989).

Fisher, E. *Catholic–Jewish Relations; Documents from the Holy See*, (Catholic Truth Society, 1999).

Fisher, S. *Revelatory Positivism. Barth's Earliest Theology and the Marburg School*, (Oxford: Oxford University Press, 1988).

Fleischner, E. (ed.). *Auschwitz: Beginning of a New Era?*, (New York: Ktav Publishing, 1977).

Friedman, M. *Encounter on the Narrow Ridge: A Life of Martin Buber*, (New York: Paragon House, 1993).

Friedrich, O. *The Kingdom of Auschwitz*, (London: Penguin, 1996).

Frymer-Kensky, T., Novak, D., Ochs, P., Samuel, D.F. & Signer, M.A. (eds). *Christianity in Jewish Terms*, (Boulder, CO: Westview Press, 2000).

Garber, Z. *Shoah: The Paradigmatic Genocide*, Studies in the *Shoah*, vol. VIII, (Lanham: University Press of America, 1994).

Godsey, J.D. (ed.). *Karl Barth's Table Talk*, Scottish Journal of Theology Occasional Papers No.10, (Edinburgh & London: Oliver & Boyd, 1963).

Godsey, J.D. (ed.). [Karl Barth's] *How I Changed My L*ife, (Edinburgh: St Andrew's Press, 1969).

Goldhagen, D.J. *Hitler's Willing Executioners: Ordinary Germans and the Holocaust*, (London: Little, Brown & Co., 1996).

Gordon, S. *Hitler, Germans and the 'Jewish Question'*, (Princeton: Princeton University Press, 1984).

Gunton, C. *The Christian Faith: An Introduction to Christian Doctrine*, (Oxford: Blackwell, 2002).

Gutteridge, D. *Open Thy Mouth for the Dumb! The German Evangelical Church and the Jews, 1879–1950*, (Oxford: Basil Blackwell, 1976).

Harries, R. *After the Evil: Christianity and Judaism in the Shadow of the Holocaust*, (Oxford: Oxford University Press, 2003).

Hauerwas, S. *With the Grain of the Universe: The Church's Witness and Natural Theology*, (London: SCM Press, 2002).

Haynes, S.R. *The Bonhoeffer Phenomenon: Portraits of a Protestant Saint*, (Minneapolis: Augsburg Fortress, 2004).

Heppe, H. *Reformed Dogmatics: set out and illustrated from the sources*, trans. G.T. Thomson, (London: George Allen & Unwin, 1950).

Herbstrith, W. *Edith Stein: A Biography*, trans. B. Bonowitz, (San Francisco: Harper & Row, 1983).

Herzberg, A. & Hirt-Manheimer, A. *Jews: The Essence and Character of a People*, (New York: HarperCollins, 1998).

Hick, J. *Evil and the God of Love*, (New York: Harper & Row, 1966).

Hick, J. *God Has Many Names*, (Basingstoke: Macmillan, 1980).

Holtschneider, K.H. *German Protestants Remember the Holocaust: Theology and the Construction of Collective Memory*, (Münster: LIT Verlag, 2001).

Hunsinger, G. (ed.). *Karl Barth and Radical Politics*, (Philadelphia: Westminster Press, 1976).

Hunsinger, G. *How to Read Karl Barth: The Shape of His Theology*, (New York: Oxford University Press, 1991).

Hunsinger, G. *Disruptive Grace: Studies in the Theology of Karl Barth*, (Grand Rapids: Eerdmans, 2000).

Hunsinger, G. (ed.). *For the Sake of the World: Karl Barth and the Future of Ecclesial Theology*, (Grand Rapids: Eerdmans, 2004).

Hyman, M. *Who is a Jew? Conversations, Not Conclusions*, (Woodsrock, VT: Jewish Lights Publishing, 1999).

Jacobs, S.L. (ed.). *Contemporary Christian Religious Responses to the Shoah*, Studies in the *Shoah*, vol.VI, (Lanham: University Press of America, 1993).

Jehle, F. *Ever Against the Stream: The Politics of Karl Barth, 1906–1968*, trans. R. & M. Burnett, (Grand Rapids: Eerdmans, 2002).

Johnson, P. *A History of the Jews*, (London: Orion, 1993).

Jones, G. (ed.). *The Blackwell Companion to Modern Theology*, (Oxford: Blackwell, 2004).

Jüngel, E. *Karl Barth: A Theological Legacy*, trans. G.E. Paul, (Philadelphia: Westminster Press, 1986).

Katz, S. *Post-Holocaust Dialogues: Critical Studies in Modern Jewish Thought*, (New York: New York University Press, 1983).

Kegley, C.W. (ed.). *The Theology of Rudolf Bultmann*, (London: SCM Press, 1966).

Kierkegaard, S. *The Sickness Unto Death*, trans. W. Lowrie, (Princeton: Princeton University Press, 1973).

Kochan, L. *Beyond the Graven Image*, (London: Macmillan, 1997).

Kanzler, D.H. *The Man Who Stopped the Trains to Auschwitz: George Mantello, El Salvador, and Switzerland's Finest Hour*, (Syracuse University Press, 2001).

Kren, G. & Rappoport, L. *The Holocaust and the Crisis of Human Behavior*, (New York: Holmes & Meier, 1980).

Küng, H. *Judaism; The Religious Situation of Our Time*, trans. J. Bowden, (London: SCM Press, 1992).

Kupisch, K. *Karl Barth in Selbstzeugnissen und Bildokumenten*, (Hamburg: Rowohlt, 1971).

Kuschel, K.-J. & Häring, H. (eds). *Hans Küng: New Horizons for Faith and Thought*, (New York: Continuum, 1993).

Lapide, P. *The Last Three Popes and the Jews*, (London: Souvenir Press, 1967).

Lindsay, M.R. *Covenanted Solidarity: The Theological Basis of Karl Barth's Opposition to Nazi Antisemitism and the Holocaust*, (New York: Peter Lang, 2001).

Littel, F.H. *The Crucifixion of the Jews: The Failure of Christians to Understand the Jewish Experience*, (Macon: Mercer University Press, 1986).

Littell, F.H. & Locke, H.G. (eds). *The German Church Struggle and the Holocaust*, (Detroit: Wayne State University Press, 1974).

Littell, F.H., Berger, A.L. & Locke, H.G. (eds). *What Have We Learned? Telling the Story and Teaching the Lessons of the Holocaust*, (Lewiston: The Edwin Mellen Press, 1993).

Lukas, R.C. (ed.). *Forgotten Survivors: Polish Christians Remember the Nazi Occupation*, (Lawrence: University Press of Kansas, 2004).

Mackintosh, H.R. *Types of Modern Theology: From Schleiermacher to Barth*, (London: Nisbet & Co., 1937).

Mallow, V.R. *The Demonic: An Examination into the Theology of Edwin Lewis, Karl Barth, and Paul Tillich*, (Lanham: University Press of America, 1983).

Mangina, J. *Karl Barth: Theologian of Christian Witness*, (Aldershot: Ashgate, 2004).

Marquardt, F.-W. *Die Entdeckung des Judentums für die christliche Theologie: Israel im Denken Karl Barths*, (Munich: Christian Kaiser Verlag, 1967).

Marquardt, F.-W. *Theologie und Sozialismus. Das Beispiel Karl Barths*, (Munich: Christian Kaiser Verlag, 1985).

Maury, P. *Erwählung und Glaube*, Theologische Studien 8, Zürich: EVZ, 1940).

Maury, P. *Predestination and Other Papers*, trans. E. Hudson, (London: SCM Press, 1960).

Maybaum, I. *The Face of God After Auschwitz*, (Amsterdam: Polak & Van Gennep, 1965).

McConnachie, J. *The Significance of Karl Barth*, (London: Hodder & Stoughton, 1931).

McCormack, B.L. *A Scholastic of a Higher Order: The Development of Karl Barth's Theology, 1921–1931*, (Princeton: Princeton Theological Seminary, 1989).

McCormack, B.L. *Karl Barth's Critically Realistic Dialectical Theology: Its Genesis and Development 1909–1936*, (Oxford: Clarendon Press, 1995).

McDowell, J. & Higton, M. (eds). *Conversing with Barth*, (Aldershot: Ashgate Press, 2005).

McKim, D.K. (ed.). *How Karl Barth Changed My Mind*, (Grand Rapids: Eerdmans, 1986).

Montefiore, C.G. & Loewe, H. (eds). *A Rabbinic Anthology*, (London: Macmillan, 1938).

Niebuhr, R. *Faith and History: A Comparison of Christian and Modern Views of History*, (New York: Charles Scribner's Sons, 1949).

Öesterreicher, J. (ed.). *Brothers in Hope*, (New York: Herder & Herder, 1970).

Pangritz, A. *Karl Barth in the Theology of Dietrich Bonhoeffer*, (Grand Rapids: Eerdmans, 2001).

Pannenberg, W. (ed.). *Revelation as History*, (London: Macmillan, 1969).

Rauschning, H. *Hitler Speaks*, (London: Thorton Butterworth, 1940).

Ritschl, D. *The Logic of Theology*, (London: SCM Press, 1986).

Rodin, R.S. *Evil and Theodicy in the Theology of Karl Barth*, (New York: Peter Lang, 1997).

Röhr, E. (ed.). *Ich bin was ich bin: Frauen neben großen Theologen und Religionsphilosophen des 20. Jahrhunderts*. Originalausg. (Gütersloh: Gütersloher Verlagshaus, 1997).

Rosenzweig, F. *Der Stern der Erlösung*, (Frankfurt am Main: Suhrkamp Verlag, 1988 repr. 1993); ET *The Star of Redemption*, trans W.W. Hallo, (London: Routledge & Kegan Paul, 1971).

Roth, J.K. & Maxwell, E. (eds). *Remembering for the Future 2000: The Holocaust in an Age of Genocide*, 3 vols, (Basingstoke: Palgrave, 2001).

Rubenstein, R.L. *After Auschwitz: History, Theology, and Contemporary Judaism*, (Baltimore: The Johns Hopkins University Press, 1992).

Rumscheidt, H.M. (ed.). *Footnotes to a Theology: The Karl Barth Colloquium of 1972*, (Corporation for the Publication of Academic Studies in Religion in Canada, 1974).

Russell, L. *Church in the Round: Feminist Interpretation of the Church*, (Louisville: John Knox/Westminster Press, 1993).

Scholder, K. *Die Kirchen und das Dritte* Reich, 2 vols, (Berlin, 1977–1985); ET *The Churches and the Third Reich*, trans. J. Bowden, (London: SCM Press, 1987–1988).

Schwarz-Bart, A. *The Last of the Just*, trans. S. Becker, (New York: MJF Books, 1960).

Schweitzer, A. *The Quest of the Historical Jesus: A Critical Study of its Progress from Reimarus to Wrede*, (Baltimore: The Johns Hopkins University Press, 1998).

Selinger, S. *Charlotte von Kirschbaum and Karl Barth: A Study in Biography and the History of Theology*, (University Park, PA: Pennsylvania State University Press, 1998).

Sonderegger, K. *That Jesus Christ Was Born a Jew: Karl Barth's 'Doctrine of Israel'*, (Pennsylvania: The Pennsylvania State University Press, 1992).

Soulen, R.K. *The God of Israel and Christian Theology*, (Minneapolis: Fortress Press, 1996).

Steyn, J. *The Jew: Assumptions of Identity*, (London: Cassell, 1999).

Talmage, F.E. (ed.). *Disputation and Dialogue: Readings in the Christian–Jewish Encounter*, (New York: Ktav Publishing, 1975).

Torrance, D.W. (ed.). *The Witness of the Jews to God*, (Edinburgh: The Handsel Press, 1982).

Torrance, J.B. *Worship, Community, and the Triune God of Grace*, (Carlisle: The Paternoster Press, 1996).

Turner, D. *Faith, Reason and the Existence of God*, (Cambridge: Cambridge University Press, 2004).

Van Til, C. *The New Modernism: An Appraisal of the Theology of Barth and Brunner*, (London: James Clarke & Co, 1946).

Van Til, C. *Has Karl Barth Become Orthodox?*, (Philadelphia: The Presbyterian and Reformed Publishing Company, 1954).

Viereck, P. *Metapolitics: The Roots of the Nazi Mind*, (New York: Capricorn Books, 1965).

Ward, K. *A Vision to Pursue*, (London: SCM Press, 1991).

Weber, O. *Church Dogmatics: A Selection*, (London: Lutterworth Press, 1954).

Webster, J. *Karl Barth*, (London: Continuum, 2004).

Young, J.E. *The Texture of Memory: Holocaust, Memorials and Meaning*, (New Haven: Yale University Press, 1993).

Articles

Brockway, A. 'The Theology of the Churches and the Jewish People', (Centre for the Study of Judaism and Jewish–Christian Relations, Birmingham, 1989). Available at www.abrock.com/Birmingham.html.

Brockway, A. 'The Churches in the Search for Middle East Peace', in *Christian Social Action*, (1996).

Conway, J. 'Christianity ans Resistance: The Role of the Churches in the German Resistance Movement.' paper presented at the Birmingham conference on *Resistance and Christianity*, (April 1995).

Conway, J.S. 'How Shall the Nations Repent? The Stuttgart Declaration of Guilt, October 1945', in *Journal of Ecclesiastical History*, vol.38, no.4 (1987).

Conway, J.S. 'The Changes in Recent Decades in the Churches' Doctrine and Practice Towards Judaism and the Jewish People', in *...und über Barmen hinaus. Studien zur Kirchlichen Zeitgeschichte*, (Göttingen: Vandenhoeck & Ruprecht, 1995).

Demson, D.E. 'Israel as the Paradigm of Divine Judgment: An examination of a theme in the theology of Karl Barth', in *Journal of Ecumenical Studies*, vol.26, no.4 (Fall, 1989).

Forrester, D. Review of *Covenanted Solidarity*, in *IJST*, vol.5, no.3 (2003).

Jansen, H. 'Antisemitism in the Amicable Guise of Philo-Semitism in Karl Barth's Theology Before and After Auschwitz', in *Remembering for the Future: Papers Presented at the International Scholars' Conference*, (Pergamon Press, 1988).

Kessler, E. 'The Jewish People and their Sacred Scriptures in the Christian Bible: A Response to the Pontifical Biblical Commission Document.' See www. jcrelations.net (2003).

Kranzler, D.H. 'The Swiss Press Campaign that Halted Deportations to Auschwitz and the Role of the Vatican, the Swiss and Hungarian Churches,' in *Remembering for the Future: Papers Presented at the International Scholars' Conference*, (Pergamon Press, 1988).

Krumwiede, H.-W. 'Göttinger Theologie im Hitler-Staat', in *Jahrbuch der Gesellschaft für niedersächsiche Kirchengeschichte*, 85 (1987).

Lapide, P. 'No Balm in—Barmen? A Jewish Debit Account', in *The Ecumenical Review*, vol.36, (October, 1984).

Lindsay, M.R. '"Nothingness" Revisited: Karl Barth's doctrine of radical evil in the wake of the Holocaust', in *Colloquium*, vol.34, no.1 (2002).

Lindsay, M.R. 'History, Holocaust, and Revelation: Beyond the Barthian Limits', in *Theology Today*, 61 (January, 2005).

Marquardt, F.-W. 'Chistentum un Zionismus', *Evangelische Theologie*, 28, (1968).

McDowell, J.C. 'Much Ado About Nothing: Karl Barth's Being Unable to Do Nothing About Nothingness', in *IJST*, vol.4, no.3 (2002).

Palmer, R. 'Eberhard Busch on "Charlotte von Kirschbaum, the collaborator" ', in the *Karl Barth Society Newsletter*, (Spring, 2000).

Shear-Yashuv, A. 'Jewish Philosophers on Reason and Revelation.' Paper presented at the Twentieth World Congress of Philosophy, (1998).

Soloveitchik, J. 'Confrontation', *Tradition*, vol.6, no.2 (Spring, 1964).

Soulen, R.K. 'YHWH the Triune God', in *Modern Theology*, vol.15, no.1 (1999).

Van Buren, P. 'Probing the Jewish–Christian Reality', in *Christian Century*, (June, 1981).

Willis, R.E. 'Bonhoeffer and Barth on Jewish Suffering: reflections on the relationship between theology and moral responsibility', in *Journal of Ecumenical Studies*, (Fall, 1987).

Wolterstorff, N. 'Barth on Evil', in *Faith and Philosophy*, vol.13, no.4 (1996).

Name Index

Subject Index